P9-DHE-082

THE REALITY OF THE KINGDOM

THE REALITY OF THE KINGDOM

*Making Sense of God's Reign
in a World Like Ours*

Paul Rowntree Clifford

WILLIAM B. EERDMANS PUBLISHING COMPANY
GRAND RAPIDS, MICHIGAN / CAMBRIDGE, U.K.

© 1996 Wm. B. Eerdmans Publishing Co.
255 Jefferson Ave. S.E., Grand Rapids, Michigan 49503 /
P.O. Box 163, Cambridge CB3 9PU U.K.
All rights reserved

Printed in the United States of America

01 00 99 98 97 96   7 6 5 4 3 2 1

Library of Congress Cataloging-in-Publication Data

Clifford, Paul Rowntree.
The reality of the kingdom: making sense of God's reign
in a world like ours / Paul Rowntree Clifford.
p.   cm.
ISBN 0-8028-0867-0 (alk. paper)
1. Kingdom of God. 2. Christianity — 20th Century.
I. Title.
BT94.C55   1996
132.7′2 — dc20   96-2477
CIP

Unless otherwise noted,
all quotations from Scripture are taken from
the New English Bible.

Contents

Preface

There are many people who find it difficult to relate the Bible to the problems facing us in the modern world. The Scriptures of the Old and New Testaments appear to be embedded in a time and culture far removed from our own, and biblical scholars often seem to be preoccupied with antiquarian research of little help to ordinary men and women struggling to come to terms with living in an environment that questions the possibility of making any sense of the human predicament, let alone of relating the Bible to it. In particular, the problem of evil seems to be an intractable one. How can anyone believe in God when the news in the press and on radio and television brings home to us in our living rooms the human tragedies that are a widespread and daily occurrence? With the trauma of natural disasters such as earthquakes, famines, floods, and tornados compounded by the human violence, cruelty, and suffering that men, women, and children have to endure, how can it possibly make sense to talk about the kingdom or reign of God? How can a loving and omnipotent God be in control of a universe like this?

Such questions brought together a group of biblical scholars in Britain to face the challenge that they were not addressing the problems ordinary people have to face. This book is one of those arising out of the discussions and the stimulation these afforded. It maintains the thesis that the kingdom or reign of God, proclaimed by Jesus, is, despite all appearances, the reality in the light of which we have to come to terms with the modern world.

My gratitude is due to Professor Robin Barbour, the convenor of the group and formerly holder of the chair of New Testament at the University of Aberdeen, who was good enough to read the first draft of the typescript and who made a number of valuable suggestions that I have sought to take into account. But I am solely responsible for the conclusions I have reached.

PAUL ROWNTREE CLIFFORD
Eastbourne, 1994

CHAPTER ONE

Fact or Fiction?

When people go to church and sing hymns like "The Lord Is King! Lift up Thy Voice," are they indulging in wishful thinking without any foundation in reality, or are they declaring how things actually are? Is it really credible to say that the Lord is King when we look around at the world as it is? With newspaper headlines featuring wars, civil strife, natural disasters, and personal tragedies, with evil manifestly rampant, does it make any sense to believe that God is governing this world? That is the question to which this book is addressed.

There can be little doubt that Jesus came announcing the imminent advent of the kingdom of God and that this was in some way inaugurated by his life and ministry. What did he mean by this, and, whatever he meant, was he mistaken or was he declaring what was actually happening and therefore how the world today is ordered? Both are questions of fact, but the first has to be answered before we can come to grips with the second. Ever since the publication of Albert Schweitzer's *The Quest of the Historical Jesus*, the questions of how and when Jesus believed the kingdom or reign of God would come have been matters of controversy, but before we ask whether or not the idea of the kingdom of God is a fantasy, we have to establish as far as we can what Jesus himself and the early church actually believed.

What is at stake are matters of fact, how things actually are, not what we or anybody else happen to think or what we would wish to be true. This point needs stressing at the present time because it has become fashionable to talk as if religion of all kinds is a purely human activity — an invention based on a variety of speculations, an option that those so inclined may choose to adopt without any bearing on how things actually are. The background of such an attitude is far wider than religion itself. In philosophical circles where the analysis of language has been a major preoccupation, the reference to anything beyond itself has been problematical. If we are caught up in linguistic games from which there is no escape, it is but a short step to say that all concepts, all thoughts, since they have to be expressed in words, are of doubtful reference to anything beyond themselves. Such a conclusion merely needs to be stated for its implausibility to be obvious. If it were accepted in its extreme form, it would be the end of science and of all knowledge except for our own thoughts and words.

A much more widespread approach and one taken for granted in many quarters is the belief that there is a clear-cut distinction between facts and values. Facts are what can be discovered through sense experience, data which can be tested, collated, and generalized, providing us with all the knowledge we have of the universe of which we are part. Values, on the other hand, are the products of human aspirations and desires that have no grounding except in human beings themselves. This entails the rejection of any objective moral standards. What is good and what is bad are nothing more than expressions of human preferences. But it is sheer unsubstantiated dogma to insist that facts are only of one kind and can be ascertained only through sense experience. If this were so, our knowledge would be severely limited. Against the background of such positivist assumptions, all religious thought and language would be a product of the imagination. Indeed, it is not surprising that an intellectual and cultural context dominated by positivist assumptions should have influenced theology.

The extreme example and exponent of this approach to theology in Britain at the present time is Don Cupitt, who in a series of fascinating and provocative books has foresworn any objective reference for Christian thought. For him religion "is not a supernatural datum. It is an ever-renewed imaginative and productive human activity."[1] In his view there are no objective moral standards, and God as a Being independent of ourselves is an unnecessary hypothesis. When we speak of God, we are really talking about ourselves, our hopes, our desires, and our fulfillment. Cupitt ends his response to David Edwards' critique of his position and his defense of his continuing to remain a priest of the Anglican Church by saying that "Anglican formularies nowhere say . . . that priests have got to be metaphysical realists."[2] This prompted a mischievous query: If Don Cupitt ordered scrambled eggs for breakfast, would he be satisfied if he were given a piece of paper containing the definition of a scrambled egg? Behind the quip lies a serious point. Is there any value in a religion that eschews all talk of a transcendent realm and remains imprisoned within a world of human speculation? Is it not more logical to abandon any pretense of being a religious believer and settle for an unambiguous humanism? That at least is a tenable position.

Very few theologians would follow Cupitt the whole way. But there are many more who start not with the discovery of objective facts but with the inventiveness of human beings. That has particular reference to the theme of this book. Christianity is based upon the belief that Jesus' birth, life, death, and resurrection were decisive not only for the human race but for the whole of the cosmos. That astonishing claim may be true or false. It may correspond to how things are, or it may be a wild and fanciful theory. It may be fact

1. Cupitt, in David L. Edwards' *Tradition and Truth* (Hodder and Stoughton, 1989), p. 284.
2. Cupitt, in *Tradition and Truth*, p. 286.

or fiction. But if it is fact, it is obviously crucial to determine as far as we can what Jesus actually said and did. That is obviously difficult to do, for we are dependent on the biblical records and their interpretation. I shall be arguing later that we have to come to terms with the fact that the data at our disposal have been shaped by the interpretation, embellishment, application, and even distortion of the New Testament writers. But the point I want to stress here is that they were responding to something that had actually taken place and that it is incumbent upon us, however difficult that may be, to try to discover what Jesus said and did, particularly in relation to the kingdom of God. Of real importance are the facts behind the writings. We may have to conclude with John Bowden, for example, that for the most part we do not know what Jesus said and did.[3] But facts there were, and we cannot rest content with a conclusion that leaves us with unanchored invention. This still leaves open the question of whether anything that Jesus said or meant was grounded in reality. But before we can begin to answer that question, we have to try to determine what facts lie behind the records.

One way of answering the questions I have raised is to take the Bible as it stands as the unadulterated revelation of God, accurately reporting, among other things, what Jesus said and did. The problem of the events behind the text is then solved at one stroke. The Bible becomes the divinely authenticated reflection of what actually happened. In its extreme form, this is the doctrine of verbally inspired inerrancy. The insurmountable difficulties in reconciling the texts with one another have led to all kinds of tortuous attempts to preserve the substantial accuracy and reliability of the Scriptures without being left with a complex of unresolved contradictions. This approach is not restricted to those who would call themselves conservative evangelicals. The pervasiveness of the basic assumption underlying the extreme conservative viewpoint is not always recog-

3. Bowden, *Jesus: The Unanswered Questions* (SCM, 1988).

nized. Throughout the church in all its traditions, the Bible is commonly referred to as the Word of God, and this readily becomes understood as the words of God. Few are sufficiently sophisticated to draw a distinction between the two, and most would be hard put to define the Word of God as applied to the Bible without equating it with the words of the text. The yawning gulf between the results of biblical scholarship and the understanding of the average member of any congregation is enormous, largely because clergy and ministers have fudged the issue and have been afraid of presenting a clear alternative to popular fundamentalism. Somehow ambiguous language has been used to paper over what is a radical difference of approach.

It needs to be said quite clearly that scriptural inerrancy and verbal inspiration are theories read into the Bible and not derived from it. The Bible itself makes no such claims. Nowhere is it said that the Word was made marks on parchment, still less printer's ink on paper. On the contrary, the prologue to the Fourth Gospel declares that "the Word was made *flesh,* and dwelt among us" (John 1:14, KJV). In other words, God has acted in events, in things that have happened, in the actual words that Jesus spoke and in the life he lived. The Bible is not about itself, but about the experience of and encounter with a whole series of events that had taken place over a specific period of time. The trouble with the conservative approach to the Scriptures is that those who adopt it will not let the Bible speak for itself. They try to make it into something which it is not in the belief that that will safeguard the faith they profess. So often the question is repeated: What are we to believe if we cannot take the Bible as an authoritative declaration of God himself? But in Michael Ramsey's memorable words in his mission to the students of Oxford, "The Bible was not rained down from heaven in the authorized and revised versions." It was the product over many centuries of a variety of authors, compilers, and editors who left behind a whole library of books, using a wide range of literary forms: story, myth, legend, history, poetry, letters, and theological reflection. It is an intensely human collection. Another way of putting it is to say that from Genesis to Revelation we have the true story of the way in which the biblical writers recorded what they believed was their encounter with the living God and the way in which they understood it.

This is not to deny the possibility of biblical inspiration. After all, if God is the ultimate reality, the Lord of history and active in the whole of his creation, he was involved in the compilation of the Scriptures. Inspiration is not necessarily to be understood as taking over the writers and using them simply as instruments in producing divine oracles. On the contrary, if God's relationship to men and women is conceived in interpersonal terms, inspiration is more properly conceived as heightening the capacity for insight. That is how J. B. Priestley described it in a very different context when he recounted his experience as a writer: "I am not claiming that a play of mine was really the work of some world-mind. This would be monstrous impertinence. The play itself, the people and scenes in it, all these are coloured and shaped by my own ego, and exhibit all my own particular weaknesses and merits. But that triumphant rush of energy and skill, enabling me to run across the dramatic tightwire effortlessly, just for this one act, was not really my own doing, and owed its existence to the fact, which might or might not be the product of chance, that this immensely greater mind could for the time being sustain my own mind. I was indeed not so much a creator myself as an instrument of creation."[4]

This is illustrated by the reported incident when Simon Peter confessed that Jesus was the Messiah, the Son of the living God: "Simon son of Jonah, you are favoured indeed! You did not learn that from mortal man; it was revealed to you by my heavenly Father" (Matt. 16:17). But this is followed in all three Synoptic Gospels by

4. Priestley, *Rain upon Godshill* (Heinemann, 1939), p. 45.

Peter being told that the Son of Man was to suffer many things at the hands of the authorities and ultimately be killed. That was not how Peter conceived of messiahship, as is evident from his reaction to the interpretation Jesus put upon it: "'No, Lord, this shall never happen to you.' Then Jesus turned and said to Peter, 'Away with you, Satan; you are a stumbling-block to me. You think as men think, not as God thinks'" (Matt. 16:23). Peter had been told that he was inspired by being enabled to see what he had seen; he had insight beyond that of his natural capacity. But that insight was defective, and in a crucial sense he was mistaken. Messiah Jesus might be, but a Messiah very different from what Peter had so far anticipated. Thus inspiration does not carry the implication of complete insight or freedom from error. It is always conditioned by human limitations.

If, therefore, the Bible does not give us straightforward answers to the questions we are asking about the kingdom of God, but presents us with the understanding and interpretation of the writers and their witness to the events they believed to be decisive, how are we to distinguish between fact and fiction, between what actually happened and what the early Christians contributed to the account they gave? Our immediate concern is not with the validity of any claims about the kingdom that Jesus or the church of the first century made. That will concern us later. What is immediately at issue is the nature of those claims.

At first that would seem to imply a straightforward examination of the evidence. But, as Lesslie Newbigin, following Michael Polanyi and Peter Berger, has recently been powerfully arguing, everyone brings to the study of any data, scientific or historical, a certain "plausibility structure." By that is meant the assumption or assumptions on the basis of which we seek to make sense of our experience. The prevailing plausibility structure in the West is the humanist assumption that we are bounded by the world of sense experience and introspection. There is no reality we can know that transcends this world, and our values, including our moral standards, are the product of our own aspirations. On the other hand, the biblical worldview has an entirely different plausibility structure. It centers on the reality of God, the transcendent Creator and Lord of history, active in the universe he has created, revealing and making effective his purpose for it. As Newbigin says, "The presupposition of all valid and coherent Christian thinking is that God has acted to reveal and effect his purpose for the world in the manner made known in the Bible."[5] Whichever is our basic assumption will influence our approach to the biblical text. If our assumption is of the first kind, we shall view the evidence in terms of the speculation of the writers. If we adopt the biblical standpoint, we shall be more concerned with that to which they were responding.

Hardly any New Testament scholars would adopt purely humanist assumptions. Even John Bowden, skeptical as he is about the possibility of knowing very much about the life and teaching of Jesus, ends his book with firm convictions about the reality of a transcendent God and the objectivity of moral values. But the influence of the humanist worldview can subtly affect our way of handling the evidence; we are prone to place undue emphasis on the inventiveness of the biblical writers at the expense of the facts that were at the basis of what they said. Similarly, the frank adoption of the biblical worldview inevitably colors the degree to which we rely on the testimony of the writers. It is important to hold our presuppositions critically and be aware of what they are.

We start by acknowledging that whatever we know about Jesus comes through the testimony of the early Christians and the churches of the first century for whom they wrote. Jesus himself left no written record, and we have no direct access to what he said and did. Moreover, the evidence at our disposal is highly selective and very limited. In recent years, much has been made of this as a

5. Newbigin, *The Gospel in a Pluralist Society* (SPCK, 1989), p. 8.

reason to be skeptical about what can be known about the life of Jesus. For example, in *The Myth of God Incarnate* Dennis Nineham cites B. H. Streeter as calculating "that, apart from the forty days and nights in the wilderness (of which we are told virtually nothing) everything reported to have been said and done by Jesus in all four gospels would only have occupied some three weeks."[6] This is underlined by the fourth evangelist, who ends his Gospel by saying, "There is much else that Jesus did. If it were all to be recorded in detail, I suppose the whole world could not hold the books that would be written" (John 21:25). But the New Testament is all that we have, and fragmentary as it is, leaving out so much we would like to know, it provides us with enough to command our serious attention and challenge our faith.

Since, then, we are wholly dependent on the texts that have come down to us, the first question we must ask is what we make of the reliability of the writers themselves, particularly the authors of the four Gospels and the Pauline letters. To what extent were they intending to record what had actually happened? To what extent were they adapting the oral and written traditions available to them to the needs of particular groups of Christians? To what extent were they speculating and imposing their own theological interpretations on the tradition they had received?

There are some New Testament scholars who seem to have become so absorbed in the details of explaining variations in the text of the Synoptic Gospels and detecting embellishments, redactions, applications, and interpretations that we might suppose that the authors had set about devising complex problems for modern scholars to unravel. That is undoubtedly a caricature. But it is surely pertinent to ask the simple question whether the authors were concerned, according to their lights, to be faithful to the tradition they had received and what they believed had actually happened.

6. *The Myth of God Incarnate*, ed. John Hick (SCM, 1977), pp. 188-89.

Luke is quite explicit about this in the prologue of his Gospel: "Many writers have undertaken to draw up an account of the events that have happened among us, following the traditions handed down to us by the original eyewitnesses and servants of the Gospel. And so I in my turn, your Excellency, as one who has gone over the whole course of these events in detail, have decided to write a connected narrative for you, so as to give you authentic knowledge about the matters of which you have been informed" (1:1-4).

Do we accept this at face value, as the expression of Luke's honest intention to do just what he said? Why should we not do so? It would surely be preposterous in the light of what Luke said to suppose that he deliberately set out to mislead Theophilus or to spin a fairy tale out of his imagination. No responsible critic would go so far as this. But Dennis Nineham reaches his skeptical conclusions about the historical unreliability of the Synoptic writers on the basis of a generalization that goes a long way in this direction. "For them," he says, "edification was a value in writing about the past at least as important as accuracy, which was in any case impossible for them, at any rate to anything like the degree to which we demand today. As they saw it, to have written an account of the past which did not conform to the religious beliefs of their time would have seemed irresponsible, whatever the evidence might be."[7] Such a specious generalization seems to me to be quite unwarranted and leaves the impression that Nineham is operating with the uncriticized assumption that the beliefs which the Synoptists held could not possibly be true. We are back to the whole question of plausibility structures to which reference was made earlier.

Luke may have been mistaken in reporting certain things as having happened or in recording what Jesus actually said, and at some points his sources may have been unreliable. But there are no grounds for questioning the honesty of his intention. And insofar

7. Nineham, in Edwards, *Tradition and Truth*, p. 200.

as he was concerned, like the other evangelists, to present his own understanding of the significance of Jesus, he was controlled by his intended fidelity to what had actually happened. H. D. A. Major in his commentary on these opening verses gives four reasons for Luke's justifying his claim to be a reliable authority: "1) That although many had written accounts of Jesus, he had striven to go back to the earliest origins. 2) That he had made use of *all* available material as far as it would serve his purpose. 3) That he had recognized the need for a high standard of accuracy. 4) That he had tried to present events in their chronological order and relations."[8] Major concludes that the text of the Gospel largely justifies Luke's claims. In particular, Major regards Luke's reference to eyewitnesses as crucially important: "St Luke, as the companion of St Paul, must almost certainly have met St James, the Lord's brother, and St Peter."[9]

The same can be said of Paul himself. In his letter to the Galatians, he tells his readers that three years after his conversion, he went to Jerusalem and spent two weeks with Peter, during which time he met James, the brother of Jesus (Gal. 1:18-20). As someone has pertinently remarked, presumably they did not simply discuss the weather! And C. H. Dodd has convincingly shown that Paul was dependent on the earliest tradition, based on firsthand witnesses.[10] Again, the Fourth Gospel, which has often been characterized as theological speculation and as being of little value for any reliable information about what Jesus actually said and did, cannot be written off so easily. To quote what I have written elsewhere, "Whatever may have been the didactic concern of the evangelist, and however much may be allowed to his genius as a theological

8. Major, *The Mission and Message of Jesus* (Ivor Nicholson & Watson, 1937), p. 259.

9. Major, *The Mission and Message of Jesus*, p. 260.

10. Dodd, *The Apostolic Preaching and Its Developments* (Hodder & Stoughton, 1936).

interpreter, there is no reason to doubt that he himself believed that he was giving a faithful account of the ministry of Jesus. At the outset of his gospel he declared that 'the Word was made flesh,' and theological credulity is stretched too far if it is maintained that he was not really interested in what did take place in the flesh. He is not just a Bultmann from the ancient world!"[11] Dodd committed himself to the same conclusion in his major book on the subject: "This revelation is distinctively, and nowhere more clearly than in the Fourth Gospel, an historical revelation. It follows that it is important for the evangelist that what he narrates happened."[12]

There is, moreover, internal evidence which supports the intended reliability of the Synoptists and which it is difficult, if not impossible, to reconcile with the supposition — and supposition it ultimately is — that "the form of the gospel traditions is narrative about Jesus but their substance is the earliest church's expression of its own self-understanding and concerns." Professor Ben Meyer, who puts the challenge in this way, argues that the evangelists recorded sayings and actions of Jesus that ran counter to the apologetic interests of the writers. He instances the baptism of Jesus by John, the "reign of God" language, and accounts of consorting with publicans and sinners.[13] We might add the cry of dereliction from the cross and the response to Caiaphas predicting an immediate coming of the kingdom (Mark 15:34//Matt. 27:46 and Mark 14:62//Matt. 26:64//Luke 22:69). If, Meyer asks, it has to be admitted that testimony running counter to the apologetic interests of the early church is to be found in the Gospels, why should it be assumed that testimony in accord with those interests is probably unhistorical? That does not settle one way or the other the question of whether a particular saying or event is to be attributed to Jesus

11. Clifford, *Interpreting Human Experience* (Collins, 1971), p. 190.
12. Dodd, *The Fourth Gospel* (Cambridge University Press, 1953), p. 444.
13. Meyer, *The Aims of Jesus* (SCM, 1979), pp. 80ff.

himself or to the apologetic speculation of the early church. But it does leave wide open the question of historicity with a presumption in favor of taking the evangelists' claim to historical integrity seriously.

This does not mean that we can read the Gospels uncritically and treat them as if they were documents produced by modern historians whose sole concern was to give an unvarnished record of the past. Even those who claim historical objectivity today, as I have already said, are involved in interpretation and bring to their study their own presuppositions. The New Testament writers, even Luke with the claims in his preface, were primarily concerned with the demands of the gospel and its application to those for whom they wrote. They were preachers rather than historians in our sense of the word. All the same, this should not lead us to the historical skepticism that has currently become fashionable. I recall a conversation with the late Professor Lightfoot at the end of one of his lectures when I was a student. At the time he was the foremost English proponent of Form Criticism, and he held the view that the gospel tradition was shaped by the Synoptists to fit the situation and meet the needs of those whom they were addressing. "People misunderstand me," he said. "They think that what I am saying leaves them with a truncated picture of the historical Jesus. The reverse is the case. He must have been at the very least the person to sustain the impression he made and the claims which were made for him. My work leaves me with a picture of Jesus much more impressive than that held by those who read the New Testament superficially." In other words, the New Testament documents are ultimately controlled by what actually happened. Our emphasis has to be on the facts rather than the fiction. It is our task to determine as best we can what lies behind the faith of the early church, which so radically affected the course of history. My conclusion is that we shall end up with a startlingly challenging proclamation of the kingdom of God, profoundly relevant to the world in which we are living.

CHAPTER TWO

The Synoptic Picture

There are two ways of reading the New Testament. The first consists of a detailed examination of the text, using all the critical tools of modern historical scholarship, painstakingly building up a picture of the early church's understanding of the significance of Jesus. As we have seen, this has led some scholars to extremely skeptical conclusions about the historicity of the events to which the evangelists in particular refer, largely due, I suspect, to what I have called the plausibility structure with which they approach the evidence. The other way of reading the New Testament is to stand back and assess its impact as a whole and then examine the text in the light of the results of critical scholarship. This too implies bringing to the task a plausibility structure, one that assumes the possibility of God having acted in some such way as the writers obviously believed he did. The first approach has the danger of failing to see the wood for the trees. The second involves the risk of failing to take the trees seriously and of manipulating the evidence because of preconceived assumptions.

There is, however, some merit in beginning with the second approach in trying to decide what Jesus meant by the kingdom, because I believe it will enable us better to assess the evidence at our disposal. For the moment, I stress again, it is not our concern to discuss whether whatever Jesus meant by the kingdom was grounded in the nature of things or whether it is relevant to our contemporary situation. That is something we will leave until later. Our immediate concern is with what Jesus actually proclaimed and meant.

Three things stand out from the general impact of the New Testament and from the Synoptic Gospels, Matthew, Mark, and Luke in particular. The first is probably uncontroversial. It is that the establishment of the kingdom for Jesus and for those who bore witness to him was the work of God and depended wholly on the divine initiative. It is not a state of affairs that human beings can bring about, though they can be participants insofar as they respond to the divine summons to live by its principles. But the emphasis is wholly on what God has done, is doing, and will do. A broad conspectus of the New Testament leaves no room for believing that the kingdom of God in the teaching of Jesus can be turned into a political or social program of our devising.

Second, Jesus clearly related the coming of the kingdom to his own role and person. He believed that he was in some sense the divinely appointed agent for fulfilling the purpose of God, and response to him and what he was saying was the condition for entering the kingdom and living by its standards.

Third, and most important for assessing the detailed testimony contained in the records, it is evident that Jesus made an impact on his immediate contemporaries with which they found it extremely difficult to come to terms. They were constantly being taken by surprise and having their preconceived ideas and expectations challenged in disturbing ways. When they and those to whom they handed on their testimony came to formulate their beliefs, they had neither concepts nor language adequate to what they had experienced. We see this in their reaction to the events of Good Friday and Easter Day. They had to come to terms as best they could with what seemed to transcend and radically challenge everything that they had previously assumed. This is reflected in the language of the epistles, which often seems to let words tumble over one another in an attempt to express what surpasses the ability of the writers to convey. Consider, for example, the ascription at the end of the third chapter of the letter to the Ephesians: "Now to him who is able to do immeasurably more than all we can ask or conceive, by the power which is at work among us, to him be glory in the church and in Christ Jesus from generation to generation evermore!" (3:20-21). This is at any rate the "larger than life" picture to which Professor Lightfoot was referring in the conversation mentioned in the previous chapter.

Bearing in mind the third of these general conclusions, we turn to what the New Testament has to say about the kingdom. There can be no doubt that apocalyptic expectations of a dramatic intervention of God to bring to an end the existing historical state of affairs and usher in the reign of God were very much in the air. Ever since the tragic end of Maccabean rule in the first century B.C., there were those in Judaism who despaired of any political solution to the oppression of their people and who looked to the direct intervention of God for deliverance. By the time that Jesus came on the scene, many, like the Sadducees, had settled for accommodation with the Roman authorities, but there were others who cherished hopes of a dramatic apocalypse. Among the followers of Jesus were certainly to be found those who believed that he had, a key role to play in bringing about at least the restoration of the glories of the Davidic age, and they were initially shattered by the crucifixion and the apparent end of all their hopes. This is reflected in the words of the two disciples on the road to Emmaus: "We had been hoping that he was the man to liberate Israel" (Luke 24:21). And again in this question: "Lord, is this the time when you are to establish once again the sovereignty of Israel?" (Acts 1:6).

Going back to what some scholars believe was the earliest letter of Saint Paul and therefore represents a primitive strand in the expectations of the church, we find him using extreme apocalyptic language: "For this we tell you as the Lord's word: we who are left alive until the Lord comes shall not forestall those who have died; because at the word of command, at the sound of the archangel's voice and God's trumpet-call, the Lord himself will descend from heaven; first the Christian dead will rise, then we who are left alive shall join them, caught up in clouds to meet the Lord in the air. Thus we shall always be with the Lord. Console one another, then, with these words" (1 Thess. 4:15-18). This, along with a similar passage in 2 Thessalonians 1:1-12, is the most explicit apocalyptic pronouncement in the Pauline letters, though there are a number of references throughout that look to a "coming day of the Lord." It is, therefore, evident that the apostle continued to expect a future advent of Jesus. Later we shall be considering why other references to the kingdom are largely absent from Paul's extant writings. What is clear is that the expectation of an apocalyptic end to the course of history remained alive in the tradition, as can be seen in the Synoptic Gospels, and it recurs in the book of Revelation, which was compiled during a period of acute persecution.

In the Synoptic Gospels the passages of chief significance in this connection are to be found in Mark 13:1-37 (par. Matt. 24:1-51; Luke 21:5-36), as well as in several parables and sayings, which on some interpretations at least are held to have the same reference.

Mark 13 and its parallels in Matthew and Luke are notoriously difficult to interpret. They are introduced by a question to Jesus about what is going to happen to the temple at Jerusalem, and he is reported to have predicted that it would be destroyed, with no stone left upon another. What follows is a mixture of predictions about the disastrous fate of the city and its temple (which actually overtook them in 70 A.D., when the Romans destroyed them and scattered the inhabitants), and apocalyptic warnings of the end of the age and the imminent coming of the Son of Man in the clouds of heaven. The latter is not an answer to the original question.

Relevant to that, according to most scholars, are extracts from what is supposed to be a document commonly called the "Little Apocalypse," which was circulated among Christians in Jerusalem shortly before the siege and destruction of the city; it contained advice about what they should do in the face of such an eventuality. "When you see 'the abomination of desolation' usurping a place which is not his (let the reader understand)" — referring, it is believed, to the desecration of the temple by the Romans — "then those who are in Judaea must take to the hills. If a man is on the roof, he must not come down into the house to fetch anything out; if in the field, he must not turn back for his coat" (Mark 13:14-16).

The apocalyptic passages about the end of the age and the imminent coming of the Son of Man go beyond this and should be treated separately or read as providing a wider context for the historical predictions.

If the three versions reached their final form before the fall of Jerusalem — and they read like predictions rather than reflections on a recent disaster of which one or more of the evangelists were aware — there seems good reason to suppose that Jesus himself foresaw the calamity which was inevitably going to overtake the city and its inhabitants and that the answer to the original question goes back to him; however, it may later have been developed in the Little Apocalypse. There is evidence elsewhere of his distress over what was happening to Jerusalem, and this could hardly have failed to lead him to predict a disastrous outcome: "O Jerusalem, Jerusalem, the city that murders the prophets and stones the messengers sent to her! How often have I longed to gather your children, as a hen gathers her brood under her wings; but you would not let me. Look, look! there is your temple, forsaken by God" (Luke 13:34//Matt. 23:37). Again Luke tells us that when Jesus came in sight of the city on his final journey, "he wept over it and said, 'If only you had known, on this great day, the way that leads to peace! But no; it is hidden from your sight. For a time will come upon you, when your enemies will set up siege-works against you; they will encircle you and hem you in at every point; they will bring you to the ground, you and your children within your walls, and not leave you one stone standing on another, because you did not recognize God's moment when it came'" (Luke 19:43-44). Whether the apocalyptic overtones of the prediction of the fall of Jerusalem in the three chapters we have been discussing are also to be attributed to Jesus is another matter. What we can say is that they were part of the tradition, tying in with the primitive expectations voiced by Saint Paul in his letter to the Thessalonians.

We turn now to other sayings and parables in the Gospels that appear to echo the same apocalyptic theme. The most striking is found in Mark, where Jesus is reported to have said, "I tell you this: there are some of those standing here who will not taste death before they have seen the kingdom of God already come in power" (Mark 9:1). These words have created great difficulties for many people because at face value they seem to show that Jesus was mistaken in what he told his hearers was to happen. The other references are all set in the context of an injunction to keep alert and watch for the sudden and unexpected.

The first of these is the parable of the faithful and unfaithful servants: "Be ready for action, with belts fastened and lamps alight. Be like men who wait for their master's return from a wedding-party, ready to let him in the moment he arrives and knocks. Happy are those servants whom the master finds on the alert when he comes. I tell you this: he will fasten his belt, seat them at table, and come and wait on them. Even if it is the middle of the night or before dawn when he comes, happy they if he finds them alert. And remember, if the householder had known what time the burglar was coming he would not have let his house be broken into. Hold yourselves ready, then, because the Son of Man will come at the time you least expect him" (Luke 12:35-40//Matt. 24:45-51).

The same theme is taken up at the end of the apocalyptic

predictions in Mark 13: "Be alert, be wakeful. You do not know when the moment comes. It is like a man away from home: he has left his house and put his servants in charge, each with his own work to do, and he has ordered the door-keeper to stay awake. Keep awake, then, for you do not know when the master of the house is coming. Evening or midnight, cock-crow or early dawn — if he comes suddenly, he must not find you asleep. And what I say to you, I say to everyone: Keep awake" (vv. 33-37). The same imagery is reinforced by the parable of the five wise and the five foolish virgins. The five wise virgins were well prepared and had brought oil for their lamps; the five foolish virgins had brought no oil and so were not ready when the bridegroom came (Matt. 25:1-12).

Finally, there is the response of Jesus to Caiaphas when Jesus was brought before him on the eve of the crucifixion. In answer to the question "Are you the Messiah, the Son of the Blessed One?" Jesus said, "I am; and you will see the Son of Man seated at the right hand of God and coming with the clouds of heaven" (Mark 14:62//Matt. 26:64//Luke 22:69). There are difficulties with the interpretation of this claim due to what are at first sight puzzling insertions in the response by Matthew and Luke. To that we shall come in a moment. But on the face of it, here we have the most explicit declaration of the imminent end of the age and the apocalyptic advent of the kingdom of God.

Evidence such as we have set out has led a number of New Testament scholars, following Schweitzer, to conclude that Jesus took over the apocalyptic expectations which were current at the time and predicted a catastrophic and imminent end to history and the dramatic vindication of the reign of God. In passing, it is perhaps worth noting that some of those who are most skeptical about knowing anything about what Jesus actually said and did seem strangely and uncritically confident that the apocalyptic vision goes back to Jesus himself and provided the framework for the whole of his ministry. However, there is substance in the claim that, if the early church held so firmly, as it obviously did, to apocalyptic expectations, it must have been encouraged to do so by what Jesus actually taught. Whether this is a correct reading of the evidence is what we now have to consider.

There are a number of sayings and parables that do not easily fit into the framework we have been sketching. All these represent Jesus declaring that the kingdom of God had come with his appearance on the scene. This led C. H. Dodd and others to speak of realized eschatology and to argue that this, not apocalyptic, was the framework within which Jesus' mission had to be interpreted.[1] Mark tells us that at the outset of his ministry, "Jesus came into Galilee proclaiming the Gospel of God: 'The time has come; the kingdom of God is upon you; repent, and believe the Gospel'" (Mark 1:15). The force of the original Greek is not easy to render into English. *Engiken*, which the New English Bible translates "is upon you," carries with it the connotation of being "right on top of you: at your very doors," and this strengthening of emphasis is justified by the use of the word *chairos* for "time" in the preceding clause. This means not simply a moment in chronological time but a crisis of crucial significance — what John Marsh once called "a time-with-its-content."[2] The same sense of immediacy is conveyed by the account of Jesus reading the lesson in the synagogue at Nazareth. Opening the scroll, he selected the passage from Isaiah: "'The Spirit of the Lord is upon me because he has anointed me; he has sent me to announce good news to the poor, to proclaim release for prisoners and recovery of sight for the blind; to let the broken victims go free, to proclaim the year of the Lord's favour.' . . . 'Today,' he said, 'in your very hearing this text has come true'" (Luke 4:18-21).

1. Dodd, *The Parables of the Kingdom* (Nisbet, 1935; rev. ed. Fontana Books, 1961).
2. Marsh, *The Fulness of Time* (Nisbet, 1952), p. 33 *et passim*.

Again, when John the Baptist sent two of his disciples to ask Jesus "Are you the one who is to come, or are we to expect some other?" the reply he gave, as they saw the results of his healing ministry, was "Go . . . and tell John what you have seen and heard: how the blind recover their sight, the lame walk, the lepers are made clean, the deaf hear, the dead are raised to life, the poor are hearing the good news — and happy is the man who does not find me a stumbling-block" (Luke 7:21-23//Matt. 11:2-6). To put this in another way, Isaiah 61:1-2 was fulfilled not simply in words but in manifest deeds that the disciples of John were able to witness for themselves.

On another occasion, when Jesus was accused of being inspired by the devil, he is said to have retorted, "If it is by the finger of God that I drive out the devils, then be sure the kingdom of God has already come upon you" (Luke 11:20//Matt. 12:28). Here the Greek word *ephthasen* is used — having an even stronger meaning of "immediacy" or "overtaking" than *engiken* does in Mark 1:15. The latter word is again used in the announcement that the seventy-two messengers were told to make when Jesus sent them into towns and villages, which the New English Bible appropriately translates "The kingdom of God has come close to you" (Luke 10:9).

All the passages referred to above are about the immediacy of the coming of the kingdom and its realization in the actual ministry of Jesus. In the light of this, C. H. Dodd offers a different interpretation from apocalyptic of those parables and sayings of Jesus that were concerned with keeping alert and watchful. Instead of taking them to be predictions of an apocalyptic coming of the Son of Man in the future, he calls them parables of crisis. Although they are clothed in apocalyptic language, he argues that the emphasis is on the breaking in of a crisis situation and the summons to be constantly on the alert. In this way he relates them to the passages we have just been discussing. Whether or not this is a forced interpretation is not my immediate concern. Later I will attempt to review the evidence as a whole. Here I simply mention Dodd's suggestion as a possible interpretation of these texts even if it represents a case of trying to reconcile the irreconcilable.

However, there are other passages, both sayings and parables, that seem clearly to portray the kingdom as having already arrived with the advent of Jesus and spreading gradually rather than breaking in on history in a cataclysmic fashion. We have only to think of the reply to the question of the Pharisees: "When will the kingdom of God come?" "You cannot tell by observation when the kingdom of God comes. There will be no saying, 'Look, here it is!' or 'there it is!'; for in fact the kingdom of God is among you" (Luke 17:20-21). "Among you" can be variously translated "in your midst" or even "within you," though the former seems the more natural rendering in the context. Again there are the parables of the seed growing secretly (Mark 4:26-29), the mustard seed that is smaller than any other seed and yet grows into a large plant (Mark 4:30-32//Luke 13:18-19//Matt. 13:31-32), and the tares and the wheat that grow together until harvest time (Matt. 13:24-30). All these, taken together with sayings about the seasoning of salt (Luke 14:34) and the leaven in the flour (Matt. 13:33), suggest a present reality of developing influence rather than a cataclysmic happening. Some critics have suggested that parables beginning with the phrase "the kingdom of God" or "the kingdom of heaven" may have originally stood on their own and that the introduction is a later redaction. The point is not really of much importance. Whether or not the explicit reference to the kingdom is original, all the passages we have been considering are about the impact of Jesus and his ministry. If his mission was the proclamation of the kingdom of God, all the parables and sayings are relevant to it.

Two other texts that have an important bearing on the subject demand attention. The first is the saying in Mark 9:1 to which I have already referred as supporting the apocalyptic expectation of Jesus and demonstrating that he was mistaken. C. H. Dodd understands this to mean that those who were listening to Jesus would see in their lifetime that the kingdom of God had already come with power, and Dodd takes this as supporting his thesis of realized eschatology: "The meaning appears to be that some of those who heard Jesus speak would before their death awake to the fact that the kingdom of God had come."[3] John Bowden is probably right in saying that this is not, strictly speaking, an accurate rendering of the original Greek because the word "already" in the translation of the New English Bible is an interpretive addition that is not present in the original.[4] But if these are authentic words of Jesus, it is not palpably plain either what Jesus meant by them or how the evangelist understood them.

This comes to focus in the puzzling reply to Caiaphas when he asked the question "Are you the Messiah, the Son of the Blessed One?" It is chiefly puzzling because of the variant readings introduced by Luke and Matthew. Luke records "from now on, the Son of Man will be seated at the right hand of Almighty God" (22:69). Matthew, following Mark, adds the words (omitted by Luke) "coming on the clouds of heaven," but he also includes "from now on" (26:64). If we were dependent on the Markan version only, it would be natural to take the reply as a straightforward apocalyptic prediction of a future dramatic intervention of God to bring about the end of the age. Why then did Matthew and Luke introduce the words that are translated "from now on" in the New English Bible? They are not the same in each case: Matthew has *ap' arti,* which has the sense of immediacy; Luke has *apo tou nun,* which can bear only the sense given in the translation. Were they producing a more accurate rendering of the tradition? In his treatment of the texts, John Robinson suggests that the note of immediacy was already implicit in the Markan version and that the two evangelists were simply bringing out the meaning of the

3. Dodd, *The Parables of the Kingdom,* p. 43.
4. Bowden, *Jesus: The Unanswered Questions* (SCM, 1988), p. 137.

original saying.[5] Or were they introducing their own understanding of what was meant by it? If so, the force of immediacy is clearly strengthened. How could they have inserted the words translated "from now on" forty or so years after Jesus appeared before Caiaphas if they believed the declaration referred to an apocalyptic climax still awaited? Perhaps they were being faithful to the sense of the original saying without attempting to reconcile it with apocalyptic expectations still held within the early church. In any case, the forms of the saying in Matthew and Luke give strong support to Dodd's thesis of realized eschatology.

This emphasis on immediacy and on the breaking in of the kingdom in the actual ministry of Jesus is reinforced by the record of his conflict with the scribes and Pharisees. Following the heralding by John the Baptist that the kingdom of God was about to dawn and calling all Israel to repentance, Jesus is portrayed as claiming that with him the prophecy had been fulfilled. He challenged religious leaders with the message that all who repented, whoever they were, would be heirs of the kingdom. This message was not restricted to those who thought of themselves as the religious elite, faithfully obeying the Torah — the Jewish law and its authoritative interpretation. Sinners — even the outcasts of society — were to be welcomed by God provided they repented. Strict observance of the law was to be replaced by open acceptance of the reign of God, and this was not the abrogation of the law but its fulfillment. Jesus, therefore, challenged the legalistic insistence of the scribes and Pharisees on a strict outward observance of such prescriptions as exact keeping of the Sabbath and rules about ritual cleanliness in the eating of certain foods, announcing an entirely new dispensation of the unmerited mercy of God open to all who would respond to his summons. His message was nothing less than the reformation and restoration of the whole nation with the crucial and revolutionary rider that with

5. Robinson, *Jesus and His Coming* (SCM, 1957), pp. 47-50.

the restoration of the new Israel, the door would be open to the Gentile world to inherit the blessings of the new age. First the new Israel, then the gathering in of the nations. The choice of the twelve disciples symbolizing the twelve tribes was to be the core of the new Israel. All this was now about to happen, though it was contingent upon repentance and readiness to respond to the summons. The day of the kingdom had come. It was already present for those with ears to hear and eyes to see.

My concern in the foregoing pages has been to pave the way for asking what Jesus actually said about the kingdom and what he meant by it. What, if anything, is directly attributable to Jesus himself and what is to be put down to the embellishment or adaptation of the early church is for the moment left an open question, though I have entered caveats against assuming that the texts are to be interpreted in the light of either presupposition.

The sharp contrast of approach to the Synoptics as a whole that John Bowden sets out in *Jesus: The Unanswered Questions* does not seem to me to be a satisfactory way of tackling the problem. Citing the American scholar John Knox, he writes, "There are those like Professor Dodd who say, 'We have no right to distrust any of the Gospel statements unless there is good cause. There is no reason to doubt the essential accuracy of Jesus in the picture offered by the Gospels, so the burden of proof lies with those who reject it.' And there are those who like himself [namely, John Knox] . . . would rather say, 'The tradition about Jesus has undergone many important changes because of the way in which the Gospels have been so much bound up with the life and faith of the first century. The Gospels tell us more about the early church than they do about Jesus. There is much in them that is more likely to have arisen out of the life and faith of the first Christians than to come directly from Jesus himself.'"[6] But when we stand back and look at the evidence as a whole in reference to the kingdom, it has two

6. Bowden, *Jesus: The Unanswered Questions,* pp. 44-45.

striking features which suggest conclusions that cut across both approaches outlined in the quotation.

In the first place, the Synoptic Gospels present no tidy framework within which all the references to the kingdom can be reconciled. The Gospels give two different pictures mixed up with one another: apocalyptic predictions about a cataclysmic intervention of God in the future, and the proclamation of the kingdom as already having come in the advent of Jesus himself. It is difficult to resist the conclusion that the Synoptists have not come to terms with the implicit contradiction — or, if not contradiction, with the way of relating past and present experience to future hopes.

In the second place, the whole of the New Testament, the Synoptic Gospels included, bears witness to the problem of coming to terms with a person and events which had had a shattering impact upon the early Christians and for which the concepts and words at the disposal of the writers were inadequate. Following Lightfoot's dictum that the Jesus of history must at the very least have been such to produce the impact he did, there are clear indications that in many ways Jesus radically challenged the expectations, the ideas, and the way of life of those with whom he came in contact.

It is, therefore, surely permissible to ask whether we can detect a person and a vision of the kingdom coming through the discoveries, perplexities, and struggles of the primitive church instead of presuming that the biblical writers were imposing their theological views and practical interests on a tradition which did not warrant them. They were testifying to someone and something greater than themselves: what they believed was a decisive disclosure of God. Whether or not they were right is another matter. But the events gave rise to the testimony. And at least we can try to see what kind of vision of the kingdom comes through it. It may on the surface appear confused, but if Jesus was the controversial figure who alone would account for the tradition that has come down to us, confusion, perplexity, and misunderstanding should not surprise us.

CHAPTER THREE

The Proclamation of Jesus

The Synoptic picture of the kingdom that I sketched in the last chapter was far from complete. It concentrated on the evidence we have of the views of the evangelists regarding its timing and dramatic character, leaving open what Jesus himself believed and proclaimed. At that stage I made no attempt to reach even a tentative conclusion about whether he shared the apocalyptic expectations that were current at the time or whether for him the kingdom had come during his ministry or whether, like the Synoptists, he appeared to combine both convictions and leave them unreconciled. Nor did I attempt to describe the content of his teaching and the sort of kingdom he proclaimed. To those matters we must now address ourselves.

What picture of Jesus comes through the Synoptic testimony? In answering the question in this form, we do not need to set aside the main results of the historical criticism of the New Testament over the past century. We cannot be sure that the actual words of Jesus have been accurately transmitted, and we have to give full weight to the interpretation, adaptation, and application of the evangelists as they sought to relate the gospel to the different situations that the early Christians faced forty or more years after the events. Furthermore, they were compiling their Gospels several decades after what came to be called·Good Friday and Easter Day. But in his recent and balanced assessment of these factors, Professor Graham Stanton of King's College, London, reaches the following "working hypothesis": "We may accept that the traditions of the actions and teachings of Jesus preserved in the synoptic gospels are authentic," adding four important provisos: "(i) the evangelists have introduced modifications to the traditions; (ii) and they are largely responsible for their present contexts; (iii) some traditions can be shown to stem from the post-Easter period rather than the lifetime of Jesus; (iv) since certainty nearly always eludes us, we have to concede that some traditions are more probably authentic than others."[1] With this working hypothesis I find myself in substantial agreement. I leave until later a consideration of the way in which the events of Good Friday and Easter in particular influenced the evangelists' perception of the kingdom. Here I am concerned with the proclamation of the kingdom by Jesus himself as it comes through the testimony of the Synoptists.

One thing can be asserted about this with reasonable confidence. Jesus proclaimed the immediacy of the coming of the kingdom of God, whether it had already started to manifest itself or whether its fulfillment was about to occur in the lifetime of his hearers. This clear note of immediacy is struck time and time again, and it could hardly have been so prominent in the three Gospels unless it went back to Jesus himself. The writers had to come to terms with the fact that expectations of immediacy had not been fulfilled, at least not in the way they had anticipated. If they had been rewriting the ministry of Jesus to conform to their own situation, they could hardly have preserved this emphasis on immediacy unless they had felt compelled to do so by the facts. This strengthens our earlier conclusion that the Synoptists have to be trusted to have been faithful to the tradition and that, to paraphrase Luke's words, they

1. Stanton, *The Gospels and Jesus* (Oxford University Press, 1989), p. 163.

were concerned to provide authentic knowledge of what had actually happened.

How much further can we go? It seems to me that, whatever Jesus believed about the ultimate future, his immediate aim and expectation was the restoration of Israel, if not in his own lifetime, then in the events that would follow upon his death. Professor Ben Meyer has argued this in persuasive detail in his book *The Aims of Jesus*.[2] The background is to be found in the various sects that emerged in Judaism after the return of the exiles from captivity in Babylon following the sack of Jerusalem and the deportation of the population in the sixth century B.C. The returning exiles set about rebuilding the temple and the walls of the city, many of them looking back to restoring the idealized age of King David before the kingdom was divided between north and south and the subsequent dispersal of the northern tribes. The ancient prophets of Israel had declared that the nation would be saved by a faithful remnant, and this too played an important part in postexilic expectations.

By the time that John the Baptist came on the scene, there were four major groupings in Judaism with different ideas about the way in which Israel could achieve its destiny. The Sadducees were the conservative party holding to the strict observance of the Torah or Mosaic law and the preservation of the ritual of the temple. They were the aristocratic elite of Judaism — what we today would call the establishment. They rejected any amplifications of or deviations from the ancient law, and for them the destiny of Israel centered upon the temple and the priestly order. Hence their outraged reaction to what Jesus had to say about the temple and his symbolic action in daring to cleanse the temple's precincts. The Pharisees too insisted on a strict observance of the law, amplifying this with detailed prescriptions about the way in which pious Jews were meant

2. Meyer, *The Aims of Jesus* (SCM Press, 1979); cf. E. P. Sanders, *Jesus and Judaism* (SCM Press, 1985).

to behave. Dependent on the scribes, who were the learned expositors, the Pharisees appear to have been a lay movement, appealing to all the people to return to strict observance of the Torah and the interpretation of it as the means to Israel's restoration as the divinely appointed nation. Those who did not conform were regarded as outcasts, and the Pharisees were particularly offended by the way in which Jesus consorted, eating and drinking, with those whom they regarded as beyond the pale.

The other two main groups were the Essenes and the Zealots, though neither were homogeneous. They were separate communities or factions to which general descriptions may be applied. The Essenes consisted of those who had given up the people as a whole as apostate and had withdrawn from society into monastic communities in the desert to preserve the remnant of the true Israel. The Zealots were the revolutionaries, convinced that only armed struggle against the Roman authorities offered any hope of the restoration of Israel's former glories. The Essenes and the Zealots played little or no part, except by way of contrast, in the drama of Jesus' ministry. His conflict was primarily with the scribes and the Pharisees and later with the Sadducees and the priestly caste. His proclamation of the kingdom was a direct challenge to much for which they stood.

Then John the Baptist began preaching in the wilderness, proclaiming the imminent coming of the kingdom of God and the fulfillment of all Israel's hopes, calling the whole people to repentance irrespective of who they were, the religious and the irreligious alike, and summoning them to submit to baptism as a sign of belonging to a nation prepared to meet its God. According to the evangelists, Jesus identified himself with those who responded to the call and bade John baptize him, saying that it was needful for him "to conform in this way with all that God requires" (Matt. 3:15).

This is the prologue to the public ministry of Jesus. He identified himself with the preaching of John, but with this difference: whereas John had announced the imminent coming of the kingdom and called the people to be prepared for it, Jesus proclaimed that in his person the kingdom had arrived. All who repented and accepted his authority could enter the kingdom; they could be witnesses to and share in God's manifest reign. Like John the Baptist, Jesus called the whole nation to repentance, including those who believed themselves to be the guardians of Israel's heritage. Neither the strict observance of the Torah and its detailed applications nor the preservation of the temple were the conditions for Israel's restoration. This now depended on a renunciation of all exclusivist claims within the nation based on the observance of tradition. On the contrary, the hope of Israel lay in dependence on the mercy of God and readiness to do his will, whatever that might be. The old era had come to an end, and a new age had dawned with the proclamation of Jesus. And, as we shall see, the nature of this kingdom that God was inaugurating through him was radically different from that which the scribes, Pharisees, and Sadducees alike conceived to be the nation's destiny. To that end, Jesus chose twelve disciples, symbolizing the twelve tribes, to be the core of the new Israel. The sole conditions for being part of restored Israel were repentance and openness to a new dispensation.

It soon became clear that Jesus' message was going to meet fierce resistance. While at first Mark was probably right in saying that "the common people heard him gladly" (Mark 12:37, KJV), the religious leaders were becoming increasingly disturbed by his influence. This is a familiar pattern. Whenever a powerful voice is raised challenging the establishment, it has an immediate popular appeal. Only when this begins to be taken seriously by the authorities do the storm clouds appear on the horizon. This is what seems to have happened in the case of Jesus. It became clear that his message about the radical restoration of Israel was not going to be heeded, and he began to talk increasingly to his disciples about the persecution and suffering

that lay ahead not only for himself but for them as well. There is
no reason to doubt that Jesus came to see his impending death as
of a piece with the inauguration of the kingdom. But he believed
that God would vindicate him and the true Israel restored. This
would lead to the extension of the kingdom to all nations, fulfilling
the Hebrew prophecies that the nations would come to acknowledge
the restored kingdom of Israel and the sovereignty of God (Mic.
4:1-4; Isa. 2:2-4; 56:7; 60:1-2).

While the proclamation of Jesus concentrated on the restoration
of Israel as the precondition of the realization of God's universal
sovereignty, there are clear indications in the Synoptic Gospels that
he looked beyond this to the establishment of a universal kingdom
to which all peoples would be heirs provided they too repented and
acknowledged the kingly role of God. Many examples can be cited:
the parables of the wedding feast, the mustard seed, and the sheep
and the goats (Matt. 22:1-14; Mark 4:30-32; Matt. 25:31-42), and
various sayings with the same implication (Matt. 8:11; 12:41-42;
13:38; Mark 14:9). Moreover, the parables of the good Samaritan
and the cleansing of the ten lepers portray the positive attitude of
Jesus to those beyond the bounds of Israel (Luke 10:29-37; 17:11-
19). Critics attribute some of these indications to reading back into
the text what later came to be taken for granted by the early church
in the light of the mission to the Gentiles. But it is doubtful, to say
the least, whether they are all rationalizations after the events. After
all, it is clear that Jesus extended his call to repentance beyond the
bounds of any elite in Judaism, and it was only a step beyond that
to proclaim God's mercy to all peoples.

The issue aroused fierce controversy in the early days of the
church. There were Judaizers among the early Christians who insisted that Gentiles should become Jews and observe the prescriptions of the Jewish law. This was not surprising, given Jesus' emphasis
on the restoration of Israel as the prerequisite of the coming of the
kingdom. But the universal emphasis prevailed, and Paul's mission-

ary journeys were the result, so that later it could be said that "through the Gospel the Gentiles are joint heirs with the Jews, part of the same body, sharers together in the promise made in Christ Jesus" (Eph. 3:6).

In recent years, much discussion has taken place about the claims Jesus made about himself and his own role in the inauguration of the kingdom. Did he claim to be the expected Messiah, or was this a title ascribed to him by the early church? In *The Aims of Jesus,* Ben Meyer makes a powerful case for the actions of Jesus being Messianic, whatever reserve he showed in claiming the title for himself. Other ascriptions such as "Son of God" and "Son of Man" were accepted in the early church, though the origin and meaning of the latter title is far from clear. Again the question has been asked to what extent Jesus saw his role in the light of the Suffering Servant of Isaiah 53. Whatever may be the answers to these questions, it is hard to resist the conclusion that the impact of the personality of Jesus was such that the early church was driven to make the claims for him that it did. At least this much can be said with some confidence: Jesus saw himself as being the representative of God in the inauguration of the kingdom and as being in the closest relationship with God in the doing of the divine will. Professor Stanton sums up the conclusion of his discussion of the titles applied to Jesus in the New Testament as follows:

> Perhaps one saying in particular may be taken as characteristic of Jesus' self-understanding: this saying is neither a claim to be Messiah, nor a claim to be a Son or the Son of God, nor a claim to be Son of Man. In Matt. 10.40=Luke 10.16 (and cf. also John 13.20) Jesus says to his disciples: "He who receives you receives me, and he who receives me receives him Who sent me." Just as the disciples are sent on their mission with the authority of Jesus, he himself has been sent to Israel with the authority of God. Jesus implies that he bears prophetic authority, but he does not appeal to particular titles. Jesus

speaks about God only indirectly as the "one by whom he has been sent," but the implicit claim which lies behind this is bold, to say the least.[3]

Indeed it is to say the least, and, given the resurrection, it is sufficient to warrant the titles that the early church ascribed to him.

The proclamation of the kingdom was the apocalypse or unveiling of the reign of God on earth. This had already begun to happen in the ministry of Jesus, and it was to continue through a period of suffering and persecution following his death and was to lead to final vindication. This was the coming of a new age. The age of the law and the prophets had ended. The age of the manifest reign of God had begun, and its promises and demands, as we shall see in the next chapter, were a revolutionary new beginning. Apart from all that Jesus said about the inauguration of the kingdom that was taking place during his earthly ministry, the Matthean version of the Lord's Prayer underlines that the kingdom was expected to come on earth, within earthly history. The Lukan version is shorter, and it is tempting to assume that this must have been the original tradition that Matthew amplified. Luke says that when one of the disciples asked Jesus to teach them how to pray, he replied, "When you pray, say, 'Father, thy name be hallowed; thy kingdom come'" (11:2). Matthew adds, "thy will be done, on earth as in heaven" (6:10). This may well come from another and even older tradition, or Matthew, as he often does, may simply be clarifying what he took to be its meaning. Whichever is the case, Matthew, who used apocalyptic language more freely than the other Synoptists, clearly understood that the kingdom was to come on earth. It may, therefore, be a mistake to suppose that Jesus' proclamation of the kingdom is to be understood as foretelling the imminent end of history, in the sense of the end of life on this planet. In any case, the "eschaton" or the end is never explicitly defined in this sense in the

3. Stanton, *The Gospels and Jesus,* pp. 233-34.

New Testament. It is a phrase imported into the discussion of apocalyptic in modern discussions.

Are we, then, to understand that Jesus expected an entirely new historical era in which God would be universally recognized as sovereign Lord? Clearly the church of the first century expected a coming "Day of the Lord" when "at the name of Jesus every knee should bow . . . and every tongue confess 'Jesus Christ is Lord'" (Phil. 2:10-11). And that was even after what the early Christians believed was the vindication of the ministry of Jesus in his resurrection from the dead. But what did Jesus expect?

It seems that during his lifetime he shared the cataclysmic expectations of a transformation of the human scene that were preserved by the first-century Christians in their looking to a coming Day of the Lord. Whether this was conceived as the end of life on this planet or an entirely new historical era is not something that is clearly addressed in the New Testament. It is a question that we may want to ask and, as we shall see, is very much pressing upon us today. How this might have been answered by Jesus and the early church can only be a matter of speculation. What seems reasonably clear is that Jesus did not know what the outcome of his ministry was going to be, and that, insofar as he conceived it as the dramatically manifest reign of God and the end of the kingdoms of this world, he was wrong. And the church had gradually to come to terms with that. The vindication of Jesus was in the hands of God and was to take a form that he had no means of anticipating.

Some people may find it difficult to accept the fact that Jesus could be ignorant of the future course of events or even mistaken in his expectations. That is due to a misunderstanding of what the church has held to be the doctrine of the Incarnation. One of the major heresies which tradition has rejected is that in Jesus the divine nature replaced the human nature and that he was essentially God in the guise of a man. Orthodox Christian teaching is that he was fully human, subject to the kinds of limitation to which we are all subject — "God divinely human," in the words of the Christmas carol. And that means that he was limited by the particular culture and knowledge of the society into which he was born. To attribute omniscience to him would be to deny his humanity.

All the evidence we have suggests that his thinking and expectations developed during his public ministry. If he began by proclaiming the restoration of Israel, he made this provisional on the repentance of the people and their readiness to accept his authority. When it became clear that this was not going to happen, he began to talk about suffering, persecution, and his own impending death. How this would work out remained hidden from him, though his intimate relation with the Father gave him the assurance that he would ultimately be vindicated, however this might be tested in the garden of Gethsemane and on the cross. The consummation of the kingdom as well as the immediate future lay in the hands of God.

The ultimate outcome of human history remains in the future, but the apocalyptic language of the New Testament has become strikingly relevant to the world in which we are living and the problems that we face. For most people in the twentieth century, including many Christians, this apocalyptic language has seemed strangely bizarre, taken seriously only by fundamentalist sects. This is the case largely because in a secular age God has been banished to the fringes of people's horizons, if not lost altogether beyond them. Nevertheless, in the years following World War II, with the discovery of the potentiality of wholesale nuclear destruction, the possibility of an imminent end to human history and life on this planet has forced itself into the public consciousness. Twenty years ago a prominent scientific technologist concluded that it was almost irrationally optimistic to count on survival beyond the year 2000.[4] Major changes in the international and political scene more recently

4. See Desmond King-Hele, *The End of the Twentieth Century* (Macmillan, 1970).

may have mitigated the awesome threat that was brought home by the Cuban missile crisis of 1962, but the possibility of total human catastrophe remains to haunt even the most optimistic secularist.

Eschatology — the doctrine of the end of things — is therefore no longer a subject of concern only to those who take the New Testament or even religion seriously. It concerns everybody. However, there is a widespread reluctance to grapple with what inevitably lies ahead. Most people run away from it, burying their heads in the sand or treating it with a kind of fatalism. You can do nothing about the future, their behavior seems to say, so make the best of the present.

When the question of human destiny is discussed, and it is recognized that humans may not survive indefinitely and may indeed have a very short future, it is surprising that the universal fact that we shall all die within a very short space of time rarely enters into the discussion. For each one of us, death is the end of history as far as we are concerned, and collective disasters like earthquakes and famines and holocausts in which large numbers of people lose their lives stand only quantitatively between the death of an individual and the extinction of the whole human race.

Grasping that fact means that the death of every individual is for him or her the equivalent of the climax of history. Those who believe that we come from dust and return to dust have no more reason to regard the extinction of the human race and the end of history as more of a disaster than the end of any individual.

For the Christian, on the other hand, the end of life here and the end of human history whenever that may be is not extinction or a catastrophe but an apocalypse: the unveiling and gift from God of something entirely new. In the words of Jesus recorded in the Fourth Gospel, the promise to the individual is "There are many dwelling-places in my Father's house; if it were not so I should have told you; for I am going there on purpose to prepare a place for you. And if I go and prepare a place for you, I shall come again and receive you to myself, so that where I am you may be also" (14:2-3).

This is the apocalypse for the individual, and, if for one, it is for all, and that is the most persuasive interpretation of what Christians have held to be the promise of the Second Coming and the Last Judgment. They mark not the beginning of a new historical age but the end of this one and the apocalypse or dawn of the eternal kingdom of God. It is not an event within history, but the end of history as we know it both for the individual and also for the human race; it is the consummation of the kingdom proclaimed by Jesus, and with it the Last Judgment.

This is the ultimate destiny of every human being, and if we take seriously the parable of the sheep and the goats (Matt. 25:31-46), in which the ultimate test is the way in which we have treated the hungry, the thirsty, the stranger, the naked, the sick, and the prisoner, who in a world where millions starve and are deprived of the bare necessities of life can claim to be free of guilt? In the end there are no sheep — only goats.

All of us, believers and unbelievers alike, stand under the judgment of God and fall short of his glory. Christians are not exempt, nor do they have any claim to be exonerated. But judgment in the Bible, while involving condemnation, is based on the redemption of the world confirmed once and for all by the crucifixion and resurrection of Christ, and in the mercy of God this is the ultimate ground of hope for all people, for "It was not to judge the world that God sent his Son into the world, but that through him the world might be saved" (John 3:17). The universalist emphasis in the New Testament on both our corporate guilt and our corporate redemption transcends all those passages that have been interpreted as according a privileged status either to those who claim to be better than others or to those who claim to merit the favor of God because of their profession of faith. Thus the Christian hope is that in the world beyond this earthly one, at the name of Jesus every knee shall bow, and every tongue confess him to be the king of glory. That is the final apocalypse — the triumph of the kingdom of God, which has to be set over against the threatened demise of every individual and the bankruptcy of the human race, which is all that secular humanism has to offer. Apocalypse has replaced catastrophe in the providence of God.

CHAPTER FOUR

The Paradox
of the Kingdom

According to the Oxford English Dictionary, *paradox* literally means "that which is contrary to received opinion." There can be no doubt that the proclamation of Jesus not only contradicted prevailing opinions at the time; it ran counter to deeply held convictions and entrenched beliefs. In this sense it was radically paradoxical. We have already seen that the inclusiveness of Jesus' call for the restoration of Israel and his consorting in table fellowship with those who were regarded as the outcasts of Jewish society brought him into direct conflict with the Pharisees and scribes. But this was not the extent of the transvaluation of values in his teaching. The element of surprise, turning upside down many assumptions that were taken for granted, was a prominent feature of his ministry.

This is evident from the parables he told as well as from many sayings attributed to him. The parables are of particular importance. They were short stories taken from everyday life designed to evoke a response or an interpretation. Unlike the details of allegories such as Bunyan's *Pilgrim's Progress,* the details of the parables were not meant to be applied to anything else, though occasionally Jesus is said to have used allegories, as in the story of the wicked husbandmen, where at every point the reference to his hearers and his own role is obvious (Matt. 21:33-43).

The parables stand on their own, apart from any interpretation or application. In several cases, in some more plainly than in others, the interpretations and applications may be due to the evangelists, though this is not to exclude the possibility that Jesus may sometimes have added an interpretation himself. A good example is the parable of the sower, to which two interpretive passages are added that may or may not go back to Jesus himself (Mark 4:3-20). At any rate, the parables themselves are in all probability stories that Jesus told, easy to remember and to hand down at a time when transmission was dependent on oral tradition rather than on written records, as it is today.

The parables challenged Jesus' hearers to think again about some of the things they took for granted and often came as a shock or surprise. They could be heard and understood in different ways, and still can, according to the presuppositions of the listener. This was brought home to me some years ago when I was giving a course of lectures at the Near-Eastern School of Theology in Beirut. I listened to the exposition of two parables as they would be heard by Arabic listeners, not unlike the kind of audience to which they were originally addressed. The first was the parable of the prodigal son (Luke 15:11-32).

To a modern Westerner, this appears to be a simple story about a father welcoming home his wayward son, the point being that God forgives and accepts the repentant sinner, irrespective of anything that he or she has done. To Arab ears, we were told, it was an immensely shocking story, contravening everything that a proper son and a proper father could be expected to do. First of all, if it had been an Arab son who had sown his wild oats and reduced himself to penury, the last thing he would have done would have been to return home and ask his father's forgiveness. In addition, the parable recounts that the father saw his son a long way off and ran to meet and embrace him. But an Arab father would never run to his son; he would wait for his son to approach him. Furthermore, when the younger son asked his father for the portion of his inheritance, that was tantamount to saying, "I wish you were dead." From an Arab perspective, the only possible response to this would be for the father to kill his son on the spot, or at least to send him away empty-handed and cut him off from his inheritance. Finally, the end of the story is all wrong. The elder brother could not simply have refused to come to the feast and sulked outside. The only natural ending to such a story would have been for the elder brother to kill his father for acting as no father should.

If this sounds far-fetched, I can only add that at the end of one of my lectures on Christian ethics in which I had discussed sexual relations outside of marriage, I was surrounded by a group of Arab students who expressed astonishment that such relations should be tolerated in British society. One of them said, "If a girl had sexual relations outside of marriage here, her father would kill her!" It is probable that many of those who first heard the parable of the prodigal son were similarly shocked. That was certainly the case with the parables of the good Samaritan (Luke 10:29-37) and the Pharisee and the publican (Luke 18:10-14), both of which were a challenge to the exclusiveness of the religious authorities and their insistence on the strict observance of the Torah as a way to find favor with God.

The second of the parables that I heard interpreted from the Arab point of view was that of the unjust steward (Luke 16:1-8). This parable has presented a problem to many today who read it as meaning that Jesus endorsed sharp practice, and the application in verse nine ("So I say to you, use your worldly wealth to win friends for yourselves, so that when money is a thing of the past you may be received into an eternal home") seems strangely forced. This was probably the curious attempt of the evangelist to make some sense of a parable that he did not understand any more than the average modern reader does. However, when I heard the parable from an Arabic perspective, a very different interpretation emerged. When the rich man discovered that his steward was defrauding him and confronted him with it, the steward did not behave as he could have been expected to do. Typically he could have made all kinds of excuses. There was a mistake in the accounts. Someone else was responsible and had fiddled with the books when he was not there. He was a sick man and had not been able to give proper attention to his work. If all else had failed, he could have brought his family and relations with him and pleaded poverty and asked what would happen to all these people if his master dismissed him. But he did none of these things that he would have been expected to do. Instead, he went away and wrote out the bills of the debtors to what may have been the proper amounts and gave them a substantial discount. In other words, he did the honest thing for the first time in his life.

The expositor then illustrated the oddness of the parable to Arabic sensibilities by relating a recent incident. The college had a contract for servicing its typewriters with a firm in Beirut. When the firm presented the bill, it was found to be double that of the previous year. When the college bursar challenged the bill, the response of the manager of the firm was that the price of materials and the cost of labor had gone up in the last twelve months. The bursar pointed out that no materials had been used and that wages had not nearly doubled in the intervening period. At the end of a long and inconclusive conversation on the telephone, the manager promised to send a man around to discuss the problem. When he arrived, he went through the same rigmarole of excuses with the bursar until honor had been satisfied by bargaining. Then he asked to be given the bill back with the admission "That was our tentative account!"

Whether this interpretation of the parable of the unjust steward was more far-fetched than that of the prodigal son is beside the point. I have chosen these examples of unusual interpretations to illustrate how differently these stories could be heard according to the experience, presuppositions, and prejudices of the listeners and also to underline the shock and offense they originally caused to those to whom they were first addressed.

Perhaps the best example of the reversal of values in the parables of Jesus is that of the laborers in the vineyard, in which those who are hired for an hour's work at the end of the day are paid the same as those who toiled throughout from first thing in the morning. Of course, this parable could be read literally, as being concerned with the question of fair wages. As such it would be disturbing to any modern trade unionist no less than to laborers in Jesus' day, though it might be none the worse for that. But in the original context and given the original intention, it surely referred to God and his relationship to people. It was not about economics or labor relations but about the generosity of God, who in his mercy treats all alike. It is impossible to merit the grace of God or to qualify for his favor, because he "makes his sun rise on good and bad alike, and sends the rain on the honest and the dishonest" (Matt. 5:45). Understood in this way, the parable was a complete reversal of the prevailing convictions of the religious authorities, who believed that those who did not strictly observe the Torah were beyond the pale and could not expect God's favor. It had to be earned; it was not an unconditional gift.

I have begun with the parables because I believe they can lay the best claim to authenticity and because they were a principal way that Jesus chose to challenge his hearers to see the novelty of the kingdom he was proclaiming. But there is much else that comes through the testimony of the evangelists. Underlying everything else, the kingdom Jesus proclaimed was not only something entirely new; it stood in judgment over the old order and indeed over every human pretension to establish a healthy and durable society. It is not Jesus who is judged in the testimony of the Synoptics and the rest of the New Testament writers. He is the judge, and the coming of the kingdom is dependent on the acceptance of him as God's appointed representative. Those who do not accept his message are under divine judgment. In his contribution to *The Religion of the Incarnation,* a volume of essays by Oxford theologians in commemoration of *Lux Mundi* (edited by Charles Gore at the end of the nineteenth century), Professor Rowan Williams, the Lady Margaret Professor, maintains that this is what is basic to Christianity. It is about the confrontation in judgment by Jesus not only with those of his own time but also with everyone ever since. "It is not," he argues, "'the Incarnation' that is the basis of dogma, but judgment and conversion worked out through encounter with the telling of Jesus' story."[1] We shall return to the question of what is basic to authentic Christianity in a subsequent chapter. Here it is sufficient to emphasize that the proclamation of the kingdom was a proclamation of judgment and was recognized as such even though it was widely rejected or ignored.

This judgment took several forms. We have already noted that it challenged the prevailing religious beliefs of the scribes and Pharisees. The kingdom was inclusive rather than exclusive. It was open to everyone in Jewish society, whoever they were — the tax gatherers, the prostitutes, those regarded as ceremonially unclean (e.g., the lepers), the poor, the underprivileged, and the outcasts as well as the rich and the socially acceptable — provided that they were prepared to repent and receive God's message. This further involved dependence on the unmerited mercy of God and recognition that his favor could not be earned by ritual observances or anything else. And the promises of God pledged in the new kingdom were offered to Gentiles as well as to Jews.

Again, outward observance of the Torah and the prescriptions of the scribes and Pharisees were no substitute for inward purity, which was what God demanded. In challenging the emphasis on the kind of food that should be eaten and the way it should be

1. Williams, *The Religion of the Incarnation,* ed. Robert Morgan (Bristol Classical Press, 1989), p. 87.

consumed, Jesus is reported to have said, "Do you not see that whatever goes in by the mouth passes into the stomach and so is discharged into the drain? But what comes out of the mouth has its origins in the heart; and that is what defiles a man" (Matt. 15:17-18).

The symbolic cleansing of the temple and what Jesus said about it being superseded were also direct challenges to the Sadducees and the priestly caste, and probably were a major factor leading to his crucifixion (Matt. 27:39; Mark 14:58). The precise meaning of the saying about the temple being destroyed and rebuilt in three days is problematic, but it seems fairly clear that Jesus declared that the task of preserving the temple and its ritual, which had been central to the concern of Judaism since the return of the exiles from Babylon, was to be replaced by the development of a purified nation. The underlying sense of this may well be preserved in the words of Jesus in the Fourth Gospel, where he says to the Samaritan woman, "The time is coming when you will worship the Father neither on this mountain, nor in Jerusalem. . . . The time approaches, indeed it is already here, when those who are real worshippers will worship the Father in spirit and in truth. Such are the worshippers whom the Father wants" (John 4:21-23). At any rate, for Jesus both the strict observance of the Torah and the ritual of the temple no longer sufficed. The new Israel was to be a nation wholly dependent on God and his mercy.

When we come to the way in which the sovereignty of God is to be exercised, we reach the sharpest contrast of all to the kingdoms of this world. After James and John had asked for privileged positions in the kingdom, Jesus is said to have told the rest of his indignant disciples, "You know that in the world the recognized rulers lord it over their subjects, and their great men make them feel the weight of authority. That is not the way with you; among you, whoever wants to be great must be your servant, and whoever wants to be first must be the willing slave of all." And the further comment is added either by the evangelist or by Jesus himself: "For even the Son of Man did not come to be served but to serve, and to give up his life as a ransom for many" (Mark 10:41-45//Luke 22:24-27). This sums up the way in which Jesus exercised his own authority. He renounced the use of force and had no sympathy with the Zealots. The Fourth Gospel clearly reflects Jesus' attitude toward his ministry in the reply to Pilate's question "Are you the king of the Jews?" Jesus is said to have answered, "My kingdom does not belong to this world. If it did, my followers would be fighting to save me from arrest by the Jews" (John 18:36). And in Matthew's account of Jesus' arrest, Peter is told to put up his sword with the words "All who take the sword die by the sword" (26:52). Moreover, Jesus' final entry into Jerusalem, when he rode on an ass, was a declaration of peaceful intent. In the Beatitudes, the peacemakers are called the true sons of God, and the chapter ends with words that are as hard to come to terms with today as when they were first uttered: "Love your enemies and pray for your persecutors; only so can you be children of your heavenly Father" (Matt. 5:44-45).

This renunciation of force and repudiation of the commonly accepted attitude toward one's enemies have been stumbling blocks to Christians ever since, and a source of agonizing discussion, particularly in this century, with its two world wars undertaken to resist aggression, not to mention the conflicts that have arisen since in Korea, Vietnam, and most recently in the Middle East, the former Yugoslavia, and elsewhere. The teaching of Jesus seems to be totally unrealistic and impossible to apply to the world as it is. Of all the facets of the kingdom that Jesus proclaimed, this seems to be the most difficult to accept and appears to make the kingdom remote and irrelevant to our contemporary problems. We shall return to this point in a subsequent chapter. Here it is sufficient to say that the proclamation of this facet of the kingdom was the most radical challenge to accepted views in the ancient world and remains such a challenge to accepted views in modern times.

Closely connected with the renunciation of force is Jesus' acceptance of the inevitability of suffering, persecution, and even death in the establishment of the kingdom. The crucial passage involves the incident at Caesarea Philippi, where Jesus asked Peter, "Who do men say that I am?" In response to Peter's confession that he is the Messiah, Jesus enjoined his disciples to tell no one and went on to say that "the Son of Man had to undergo great sufferings, and to be rejected by the elders, chief priests, and doctors of the law; to be put to death, and to rise again three days afterwards."[2] This was too much for Peter, who could not accept such an outcome as the Messianic vocation. The same incident is recorded in all three Gospels and has been widely held by critics in recent times to be a post-Easter reading back into the narrative of the belief of the early church. It is probable that the form of the passage has at least been amplified and interpreted by the Synoptists, but it is another question whether it refers to an original incident in which Jesus told his disciples of his impending suffering and death. Many critics have a predilection to read back everything they can from the post-Easter faith of the early church, and this can be overdone. If we look for a coherent picture of the ministry of Jesus coming through the testimony of the Synoptists, we find that the fact that Jesus saw his impending rejection, suffering, and death as inevitable makes sense of the record once we take a holistic view of the evidence.

There are other features of the kingdom proclaimed by Jesus that would have come as a shock, if not an affront, to his contemporaries and are a challenge to the assumptions of many today. For Jesus, riches in the sight of God did not confer status in society. On the contrary, they were more likely to be an obstacle to entrance into the kingdom of God.[3] Furthermore, when the disciples asked

---

2. Mark 8:27-33; Luke 9:18-22; Matt. 16:16-19. For a detailed reference to the controversial view that the longer Matthean version is original, see Meyer, *The Aims of Jesus* (SCM Press, 1979), pp. 185-97.

3. Mark 10:23. Cf. the parable of Dives and Lazarus in Luke 16:19-31.

Jesus who was greatest in the kingdom of God, he set a child in front of him, saying, "Unless you turn round and become like children, you will never enter the kingdom of Heaven. Let a man humble himself till he is like this child, and he will be the greatest in the kingdom of Heaven" (Matt. 18:1-3). That is not how most adults think of children. Even Paul could write dismissively, if not disparagingly, of having put away childish things (1 Cor. 13:11). Many people today have either a sentimental or a patronizing attitude toward children. However, Jesus saw in them the qualities of simplicity and trust that were essential for entrance into the kingdom he proclaimed. Finally, Jesus' attitude toward women was unconventional, to say the least. In spite of the paucity of the evidence, what we have shows that women played a significant part in his ministry, and no small part of what he had to say was revealed to them.

In short, the proclamation of the kingdom in the context of Jesus' ministry as a whole was a radical challenge to entrenched and accepted assumptions. Moreover, it stands in judgment of the kingdoms of this world of all time.

CHAPTER FIVE

The Transformation
of the Kingdom

So far our concern has been to see what picture of the kingdom as proclaimed by Jesus during his earthly ministry comes through the testimony of the Synoptic Gospels. We have, as much as possible, kept to the periphery the effect that the events of Good Friday and Easter Day had on the perception of the evangelists, though we have had to reckon with the fact that all they recorded about the actual lifetime of Jesus was seen and interpreted in the light of these events. We must now try to come to grips with the radical difference that Good Friday and Easter Day made to the primitive church's perception of the kingdom.

After all, the Synoptic Gospels were compiled some forty years subsequent to these events, and while they may embody traditions that go back to those who were firsthand witnesses, like Peter and James, the brother of Jesus, they are not themselves the earliest recorded testimony of what the first Christians made of the crucifixion and resurrection. This is to be found chiefly in the letters of Paul and what appear to be the earliest summaries of Christian preaching in the sermons of Peter preserved in the Acts of the Apostles.

Here we are faced with a problem. Nobody who reads the New Testament carefully can fail to be struck by the scanty references to the kingdom in the Pauline epistles and indeed to anything Jesus said and did during his earthly ministry. Of course, we have only those few letters that are extant. We do not know what else Paul wrote or taught when he was in Jerusalem or when he was engaged in his remarkable mission to the Gentile world. But any argument from silence is notoriously suspect for the historian. We have to take the very limited material at our disposal and see what we make of it.

It is not the case that references to the kingdom are wholly absent from Paul's letters. Nevertheless, apart from the apocalyptic passages in 1 Thessalonians 2, which, as we have seen, reflect expectations alive in the early church, and a number of references to the coming day of the Lord (e.g., 1 Cor. 4:5; 7:29; 10:11; 15:51; 16:22; 2 Cor. 1:14; Phil. 1:6, 10; 1 Thess. 5:23; 2 Thess. 1:10), there are only seven — possibly eight — explicit mentions of the kingdom in those letters that are generally attributed to the apostle himself. The first of these is to be found in Romans 14:17, which is in the passage where Paul deals with the pastoral problem of what Christians should do about eating meat regarded by some as unclean: "The kingdom of God is not eating and drinking, but justice, peace, and joy, inspired by the Holy Spirit." The second is in 1 Corinthians 4:8, where the word is used, but in oblique reference, if reference at all, to the kingdom of God. Here Paul is defending his apostleship against those in Corinth who had arrogated to themselves serious authority: "You have come into your kingdom — and left us out. How I wish you had indeed won your kingdom; then you might share it with us!" The third comes later in the same chapter where, addressing the same "self-important people," he says, "The kingdom of God is not a matter of talk, but of power" (v. 20). The fourth is still in the same chapter, where Paul warns that "no fornicator or idolator, none who are guilty either of adultery or of homosexual perversion, no thieves or grabbers or drunkards or slanderers or swindlers, will possess the kingdom of God" (1 Cor. 6:9-10). The fifth mention occurs several chapters later. In the context of expounding the significance of the resurrection, Paul declares that "flesh and blood can never possess the kingdom of God," linking this with the apocalyptic expectation that he told the church in Thessalonia to anticipate. And the whole letter is brought to its climax with the invocation "*Marana tha* — Come, O Lord!" (1 Cor. 16:22). Then there are two references to the kingdom in the letters to the Thessalonians. The first of these is in 1 Thessalonians 2:12, where Paul calls upon his readers "to live lives worthy of the God who calls you into his kingdom and glory," and the second echoes the same injunction to be "worthy of the kingdom of God" (2 Thess. 1:5). Finally, there is the ascription of praise in Colossians 1:11-13 (a letter that many scholars attribute to Paul): "May he strengthen you, in his glorious might, with ample power to meet whatever comes with fortitude, patience, and joy; and to give thanks to the Father who has made you fit to share the heritage of God's people in the realm of light. He rescued us from the domain of darkness and brought us away into the kingdom of his dear Son, in whom our release is secured and our sins forgiven."

These few scattered references do not tell us very much. Taken in conjunction with anticipations of a coming day of the Lord, they indicate that Paul had embraced the teaching of Jesus about the kingdom and that in some sense the early Christians had entered into it. This is clear from the way in which his pastoral counsel is set within the context of what it means to be in the kingdom — as, for example, in Romans 14:17, 1 Thessalonians 2:12, and Colossians 1:11-13. There is, therefore, some evidence that he understood the kingdom in the sense of what C. H. Dodd calls realized eschatology. At the same time, it is equally clear that he continued to look to a day of the Lord which was still in the future, and that is the context within which present living in the kingdom had to be understood.

However, in his letters his main concern — apart from pastoral counseling and dealing with "ad hoc" problems that had arisen in the early churches — was with what he believed to be the crucial significance of the crucifixion and resurrection of Jesus. That had radically transformed the whole picture. No longer could the kingdom be understood solely in terms of whatever Jesus had proclaimed during his earthly ministry. That had now to be interpreted in the light of his resurrection from the dead.

It cannot be too strongly stressed that unless something like Paul's convictions had taken over after the crucifixion, the teaching of Jesus about the kingdom would quickly have been forgotten. Even the material in the Synoptic Gospels, on which critics of the liberal school worked to discover a wandering rabbi behind the theological constructs of Paul and the early church, would never have survived. It would never have been compiled! The Synoptic Gospels have to be read in the light of the faith of the primitive church. The fundamental mistake of the liberal critics was to approach the New Testament the other way around, reading the testimony of the early Christians in the light of what they believed they could find out about the earthly ministry of Jesus rather than reading it in an attempt to discover the significance of his ministry through the apostolic witness.

The death blow to the old quest for the Jesus of history was delivered by C. H. Dodd (among others) in his seminal book *The Apostolic Preaching and Its Developments.*[1] He maintained that in Paul's letters, as well as in the sermons of Peter in the Acts of the Apostles, we have the earliest Christian tradition, going back to the initial reaction to and interpretation of the events that gave rise to everything that followed. The evidence for this is found in citations of the original tradition that appear to reflect its use for catechetical purposes. The sermons of Peter can be summarized under eight headings: (1) This is the age of fulfillment (Acts 2:16; 3:18, 24);

---

1. Dodd, *The Apostolic Preaching and Its Developments* (Hodder & Stoughton, 1936).

(2) Jesus went about doing good (Acts 2:22); (3) He was crucified (Acts 2:23; 3:13-14); (4) He rose from the dead (Acts 2:24-31; 3:15; 4:10); (5) He is exalted Lord and Christ (Acts 2:33-36; 3:13; 4:11); (6) The Holy Spirit in the church is the sign of Christ's present power and glory (Acts 2:33; 5:32); (7) The consummation will be his return (Acts 3:21); (8) Therefore, repent (Acts 2:38-39).

The key passages in the Pauline epistles are 1 Corinthians 11:23-26 and 1 Corinthians 15:3-7. In the first, Paul records, "The tradition which I handed on to you came to me from the Lord himself: that the Lord Jesus, on the night of his arrest, took bread and, after giving thanks to God, broke it and said: 'This is my body, which is for you; do this as a memorial of me.' In the same way, he took the cup after supper, and said: 'This cup is the new covenant sealed by my blood. Whenever you drink it, do this as a memorial of me.' For every time you eat this bread and drink the cup, you proclaim the death of the Lord, until he comes." From this it is clear that Saint Paul was dependent on the tradition of the Last Supper, which was also recorded in the Gospels. The second passage is still more important as a summary of the core of the primitive church's faith: "I handed on to you the facts which had been imparted to me: that Christ died for our sins, in accordance with the scriptures; that he was buried; that he was raised to life on the third day, according to the scriptures; and that he appeared to Cephas, and afterwards to the Twelve. Then he appeared to over five hundred of our brothers at once, most of whom are still alive, though some have died. Then he appeared to James, and afterwards to all the apostles." We can hardly get back any further to the original testimony to what was believed to have happened on what came to be described as Good Friday and Easter Day.

Paul's interpretation of the theological significance of these events is found throughout his letters, though perhaps it is most fully developed in his letter to the Colossians. But whatever we make of his theology, there can be no doubt that it was based upon the earliest testimony of firsthand witnesses. The crucifixion of Jesus and the days succeeding it made a radical difference to the way in which the first Christians looked back on his ministry. The proclamation of the kingdom could now no longer be interpreted except in the light of the climax of his earthly life. That is sufficient explanation for the scattered references to the kingdom in the Pauline epistles. The promise of the kingdom had been sealed and transformed by the crucifixion and the resurrection.

This is the context within which the Four Gospels were subsequently compiled. It has often been pointed out that if they had been intended as straight biographies, such a disproportionate amount of space would not have been devoted to the last week in the life of Jesus. Indeed, it is clear that the whole of the Gospels is overshadowed by the cross, and that all the incidents selected for the record were chosen to illuminate the ultimate triumph of the crucified and risen Lord. The ministry of John the Baptist and the proclamation of Jesus that followed were not just unfulfilled prophecies. They had been vindicated in the climactic events.

All this is made completely explicit in the Fourth Gospel. Here Jesus is presented as having entered into his glory, the key word in the evangelist's vocabulary. Although the kingdom is only mentioned twice, it is plain that for the author it had already come. Jesus was glorified, reigning over the whole world. Participation in it was conditional upon a radical spiritual transformation — a reflection of the call to repentance first heralded by John the Baptist and central to everything that Jesus proclaimed: "In truth, in very truth," said Jesus to Nicodemus, "unless a man has been born over again he cannot see the kingdom of God. . . . In truth I tell you, no one can enter the kingdom of God without being born from water and spirit" (John 3:3-5). The other reference is in the scene of the trial before Pilate, already referred to in the last chapter, where Jesus says, "My kingdom does not belong to this world. If it did, my followers would be fighting to save me from arrest by the Jews.

My kingly authority comes from elsewhere." There follows the interrogation by Pilate about this claim to kingship, from which the evangelist makes plain that the kingdom of which Jesus speaks is to be understood as supervening upon the kingdoms of this world. It is of a different order and is grounded in the true state of things. By implication, the political kingdoms of this world are judged to be ephemeral, reflecting the attempts of man to rule where God actually reigns. This account of the confrontation of Pilate by Jesus — for that is what it is, not the other way around — will be of particular significance when we come to discuss how the New Testament picture of the kingdom bears on the situation we face in the modern world.

So far the stage we have reached in developing the argument of this book is a strictly limited one. We have not yet come to the point of asking whether or not the claims that Jesus made and that were made on his behalf by the primitive church are credible. The only point I have tried to establish is that the impact he made and the climax of his life on earth led the primitive church to believe and proclaim that the course of history had been radically changed. At the very least they believed that a new era had dawned and that the world had been turned upside down. It is not possible to reduce this to or extract from it the picture of a wandering rabbi who taught certain moral precepts or enunciated certain religious ideas that may have lasting validity. The claims went far beyond this.

Their nature is vividly portrayed in G. K. Chesterton's *Everlasting Man,* which is often judged to be his literary masterpiece. The question to which he addresses himself in the second part of his book is whether the coming of Christ, his life, death, and resurrection, actually transformed not only the human scene but the very structure of the universe. Was it a cosmic event of decisive significance, as expounded in Paul's letter to the Colossians? Chesterton is in no doubt about the answer. In a memorable sentence, he describes it as "That incredible interruption, as a blow that broke the very backbone of history."[2] Some idea of the vividness and originality of his development of this theme is indicated by the following quotation from his retelling of the Easter story: "On the third day the friends of Christ coming at day break to the place found the grave empty and the stone rolled away. In varying ways they realized the new wonder; but even they hardly realized the world had died in the night. What they were looking at was the first day of a new creation, with a new heaven and a new earth; and in the semblance of a gardener, God walked again in the garden, in the cool not of the evening but the dawn."[3] Or again, in his account of the birth of Jesus in a cave, Chesterton turns upside down the medieval theater for mystery plays, with its three-story stage representing heaven, earth, and hell, by portraying heaven in the cave under the earth: "The old Trinity was of father, mother and child and is called the human family. The new is of child, mother and father and has the name the Holy Family. It is in no way altered except in being entirely reversed; just as the world which is transformed was not in the least different, except in being turned upside down."[4]

This astonishing claim is either true or false. It is either a fanciful theory or a graphic description of how things actually are, whether or not anyone sees and believes it. That is what is really at stake. In the previous chapter I referred to Professor Rowan Williams' contention that what is basic to Christianity is the dogma of judgment and conversion. Anglican theology as a whole has tended to treat the doctrine of the Incarnation as basic and has maintained that to sit loosely to this is to abandon what is essential. Williams disagrees. For him the doctrine of the Incarnation and its working out depend

2. Chesterton, *The Everlasting Man* (Burns & Oates, 1925; repr. Burns & Oates, 1956), p. 268.

3. Chesterton, *The Everlasting Man,* p. 212.

4. Chesterton, *The Everlasting Man,* p. 54.

on the recognition that the proclamation of the kingdom and the apostolic testimony rest on the conviction that God's judgment on the world has been declared in Jesus and that the whole of subsequent history has to be assessed and understood in the light of that fact. I have no quarrel with this step beyond and behind the doctrine of the Incarnation. It was the main theme of the previous chapter. But I would go further. For the Reformers, divine judgment was based on what God had actually done in the crucifixion and resurrection of Jesus; therefore, if we are to understand what is basic and indispensable to authentic Christianity, it is to the dogma of redemption that we must look. Judgment in the Bible is not to be simply equated with condemnation. When the elders of a Hebrew village sat at the gates to deliver judgment for those who came to them with quarrels and complaints, their function was not merely to condemn the guilty and assess punishment but to put things right that had gone wrong. On the infinitely larger canvas of God's judgment of the world, the Fourth Gospel declares, "God sent not his Son into the world to condemn the world; but that the world through him might be saved" (John 3:17, KJV). The actual redemption of the world through the life, death, and resurrection of Jesus is what lies at the heart of the apostolic testimony. This does not imply any particular doctrine of the atonement. Of course, that was developed by Paul and other New Testament writers. But whatever they and subsequent theologians have to say about this is dependent on the conviction that the world has actually been redeemed, however that might be explained. As R. W. Dale said many years ago, "It is not the doctrine of the death of Christ that atones for human sin, but the death itself."[5]

Karl Barth developed the same theme at length in the later volumes of his *Church Dogmatics*. He asserted that the death of Jesus

5. Dale, quoted by Scott Lidgett in *The Spiritual Principle of the Atonement* (Charles H. Kelly, 1897), p. 220.

on the cross was the reconciliation of fallen humanity to God, that
this was achieved for all people at all times, whether or not they
recognized and believed it. It was a fact rooted and grounded in a
once-and-for-all historical event. Christian faith is then to be understood not as an option among a number of alternatives but as
an awakening to how things really are.[6]

To take the implications of this dogma further — for dogma it
is as a basic given on which theologians have to work by way of
elucidation and interpretation in formulating doctrine — it is in-
structive to go back to Chesterton and his fascinating discussion of
myth in *The Everlasting Man*. He maintains that mythology is a
search: the imaginative attempt to give some account of the Transcendent that is embodied in all human experience. The basic meaning of *myth* is "a story that conveys or leads to some insight into
the nature of things." The opening chapters of Genesis that tell the
story of creation are a good example of religious myth. They are
not a scientific or historical account of how the universe came into
being, but an imaginative way of expressing the insight that the
universe is dependent on God for its existence. Chesterton extends
the meaning of the word *myth* from its basic sense of story to cover
all human attempts to express what is beyond the bounds of de-
scriptive language, and his treatment of the major world religions
is within the context of mythology: all of them involve a genuine
search for the God whom human beings, in the Pauline phrase,
"ignorantly worship." This includes Christianity no less than
Judaism, Islam, Buddhism, Hinduism, and all the many different
religions that have emerged over the course of time.[7]

In this broader sense, the Bible and the development of Christian doctrine down the centuries abound in myths that are none-
theless valuable for being so, as they illuminate the search for truth

6. Barth, *Church Dogmatics* (T. & T. Clark, 1956-62).
7. Chesterton, *The Everlasting Man*, p. 173.

and lead to genuine insights. Sometimes they have to be discarded altogether when they conflict with experience or the acquisition of fresh knowledge. An example of this is the Old Testament myth of the warrior God, the Lord of hosts, who destroys the armies of Israel's enemies. Although this myth has persisted down the centuries and is still operative in many popular contemporary religious beliefs, it has to be rejected. Any dispassionate survey of the course of history compels us to discard it, whatever the value of its intentions. Its truth lies in the search for the Lord of history whose purpose is brought to fulfillment in the establishment of the chosen people, but the way in which he accomplishes that purpose is contradicted by the coming of Jesus and the kingdom that he proclaimed. Another example is the dogma of scriptural inerrancy, which, as we saw earlier, is a claim that the Bible never makes for itself and that is contradicted by the way in which it is now known the Bible came to be written. Yet the dogma of scriptural inerrancy enshrines the quest for religious certainty even if it looks for that in the wrong place and so has to be discarded.

The use of myth to explore religious experience was in some way paralleled by the late Ian Ramsey in his development of what he called models and qualifiers in religious discourse. He expounded this concept in the Whidden Lectures he gave at McMaster University in Canada[8] and amplified it in several books and articles. Taking familiar models from everyday life, he pressed their use to the limits in the search for God, qualifying them to the point where they broke down altogether, at which point he claimed that "a disclosure situation" could occur or "the penny could drop" and we could begin to recognize the Transcendent breaking in upon us. One of the examples he chose was the familiar hymn "How Sweet the Name of Jesus Sounds in a Believer's Ear." In the fourth verse, Jesus is invoked as "Shepherd, Guardian, Friend" and "Prophet, Priest, and King." All

8. Ramsey, *Models and Mystery* (Oxford University Press, 1964).

these are models the meaning of which we can identify from everyday experience, but when pressed into service to speak of Jesus, they all prove to be inadequate and have to be qualified in their application and break down "because we find ourselves wanting to say more which none of these titles, taken separately or together, will satisfy."[9] Perhaps an even better example is Ramsey's theological rehabilitation of the Victorian children's hymn "There's a Friend for Little Children above the Bright Blue Sky," which most modern hymnals exclude as being too naive for modern boys and girls. But Ramsey draws attention to the radical qualifiers in the hymn:

> A friend who *never* changeth,
> Whose love can *never* die.
> *Unlike* our friends by nature
> Who change with changing years,
> This friend is *always* worthy,
> The precious name he bears.

And he treats the second verse in the same way:

> There's a home for little children
> Above the bright blue sky; . . .
> *No* home on earth is like it
> Nor can with it *compare*.
> For *everyone* is happy,
> Nor can be happier there.[10]

However, the use of these images is subject to severe limitations, whether the images are in the form of models or myths, for they start from common human experience in the search for God. That is where we *have* to start, according to Professor Maurice Wiles in

9. Ramsey, *Models and Mystery*, p. 55.
10. Ramsey, *Christian Discourse: Some Logical Explorations* (Oxford University Press, 1965), p. 72.

his contribution to Morgan's volume based on *Lux Mundi,* to which I have earlier referred.[11] But the trouble is that if we start with human experience and the myths or models that are the product of our imagination, we may never get beyond them. This, of course, would be denied by Ramsey with his "disclosure situations" and also by Wiles and other radical theologians who believe that we do encounter the Transcendent in our everyday experience. But this depends on an ultimate belief in the reality of God and that he does come to meet us in our experience of the world. That in turn depends on the belief that God is active in his creation, disclosing himself to us in sometimes surprising ways. He is not just there to be discovered at the end of our search. The danger of starting with our experience, as I have said, is that we may find ourselves imprisoned within our myths, and the end of that road is where Don Cupitt seems to have landed with his nonrealist interpretation of religious language, his denial of the objectivity of God, and his conclusion that religion "is not a supernatural datum" but "an ever-renewed imaginative and productive human activity."[12]

To return to Chesterton, he begins at the pole opposite to human experience — with God and what God has done. He was convinced that the life, death, and resurrection of Jesus are not myths in the sense in which he used the word. They are facts — a divine initiative and intervention by which the world was actually changed. If it is true that God through Jesus redeemed the world and established his kingdom, that is as much a fact as that Jesus lived and was crucified. Of course, it is open to anyone to say that this too is a myth, and in the rest of this book we shall be considering how far a claim such as Chesterton's illuminates our human situation

11. Wiles, "The Incarnation and Development," in *The Religion of the Incarnation,* ed. Robert Morgan (Bristol Classical Press, 1989), pp. 74-84.

12. Cf. David L. Edwards, *Tradition and Truth* (Hodder & Stoughton, 1989), p. 284.

and justifies the conviction that God reigns, that his kingdom is established and is actually in our very midst. It is one thing to clarify what the claim is; it is another to be persuaded that it makes sense, that it illuminates our situation, and that there are evident signs that it is substantiated by how things actually are. The question we shall be asking is whether the kingdom of God has been manifested for those with eyes to see and ears to hear.

CHAPTER SIX

Not of This World

If it is claimed that the kingdom of God was in fact established on earth by the life, death, resurrection, and ascension of Jesus, this question arises: How can this possibly make sense or even be believable in the kind of world in which we live? That is not only a problem for us; it was no less a problem for the early church. The expected dramatic intervention of God to bring all things into subjection to him had not taken place; the world continued as it had been in the past, and the events surrounding the life of Jesus of Nazareth were at most a matter of passing curiosity for some people and were totally ignored by the vast majority. The hope still persisted among the first Christians that this would yet be changed by a dramatic divine intervention, but the hope began to fade as the intervention did not occur, and the church had to come to terms with a wholly unexpected way in which the kingdom of God had to be proclaimed in a world governed by entirely different assumptions.

Our problem is essentially the same. Insofar as people today claim to believe in God, for the most part they expect him to act in much the same way that people expected him to act in ancient Palestine. If he is the omnipotent God of love who rules the world, surely he should be expected to intervene to prevent wars, to avert catastrophes like earthquakes, famines, and natural disasters, and to remove the threat of all forms of evil and suffering. And there are those who go so far as to justify this expectation by pointing to remarkable events such as the escape of the British armies from Dunkirk in World War II and other examples of dramatic interventions that are claimed to be instances of divine providence.

This will not do. Facts have to be faced. If the escape from Dunkirk was an example of divine providence, why didn't God intervene to avert the Holocaust and rescue tens of thousands from the Nazi concentration camps? Why was Stalin allowed to exercise his tyranny and condemn countless men, women, and children to suffering and death? Why are there earthquakes, famines, and all kinds of natural disasters? Some of the suffering that people endure is due to the cruelty and greed of others, but even then the question arises why an all-powerful and loving God should allow them to have the freedom to wreak such havoc. But perhaps natural disasters cry out most for divine justification, since they are not attributable to malign human agency.

If, then, we are to make any sense of the claim that Jesus established the kingdom of God not only in first-century Palestine but for the whole world in every age, including our own — and this is the issue with which we began this study — we have to face the fact that in doing so he confounded all natural human expectations. Not only did he contradict the expectations of ancient Judaism and the primitive church that first came to birth in a Jewish context, but he has similarly contradicted the expectations of every age, including our own. Either we have to deny the claim that the kingdom of God has any substance in the light of the kind of world in which we live, and so consign it to the realm of fantasy and fairy tales, or we have to start elsewhere, with the totally unexpected that challenges all human assumptions and compels us to face the possibility that God's ways are not our ways nor his thoughts our thoughts.

This is the situation in which the apostles found themselves in the first century. They had to come to terms with the failure of Jesus to fulfill their expectations and begin to realize that the kingdom he proclaimed and inaugurated was not of this world in the sense that it did not conform to natural human expectations. It did not do so during the public ministry of Jesus, which as we have seen is evident from his conflict with the religious leaders of the day. Nor did it conform to the expectations of his own disciples. This is plain from their reaction to what he began to tell them about his impending suffering and death. That contradicted all their hopes about the kingdom and the restoration of Israel. The totally new perspective that this implied came into focus in the confrontation of Jesus with Pilate, when, according to the Fourth Gospel, Jesus was asked whether he claimed kingship for himself. "My kingdom does not belong to this world," he answered. "If it did, my followers would be fighting to save me from arrest by the Jews. My kingly authority comes from elsewhere."

That constituted the problem for the early church after the crucifixion and the resurrection. How were they to maintain the sovereignty of God in the light of what had happened? And the same is our problem today.

Before we look at the ways in which earlier believers tried to maintain the sovereignty of God and the difficulties to which the different solutions gave rise, it may be helpful to clarify further the major issue at stake by referring to a difficult and somewhat obscure section of Karl Barth's *Church Dogmatics* in which he expounds the theme of Jesus as the light of the world.[1] Barth maintains that if we are to understand God's providence, we must look not to nature or our ordinary human experience but to the light of Jesus' unique revelation. He does not deny that there are lesser lights to be discerned in the world as we experience it, but he argues that we will

1. Barth, *Church Dogmatics* (T. & T. Clark, 1961), IV.3.1, pp. 151-65.

be led astray if we start there; for these lights are obscure and of themselves puzzling. They are to be interpreted only in the light of the revelation incarnated in Jesus. In other words, that revelation embodied in the proclamation, death, resurrection, and ascension of Jesus is the declaration of how things actually are; it is the way in which God rules the world, and our experience of the world as it is can be illuminated only in that light. Barth goes on to argue that what he calls the lesser lights, of which the orderly structure of the universe is the principal example, are to be interpreted in the true light of the Christian revelation. This does not resolve the mystery of evil and suffering as we encounter it in our everyday experience. Barth's contention is that we begin to make sense of the context in which we live only when we recognize that the kingdom of God is the reality which alone illuminates that context and with it the contradictions of the kingdoms of this world. Jesus is the one true light. In the words of the Fourth Gospel, "All that came to be was alive with his life, and that life was the light of men. The light shines on in the dark, and the darkness has never mastered it. . . . The real light which enlightens every man was even then coming into the world" (John 1:3-5, 9).

If that is the premise with which we have to start, the question then arises how the kingdom of God is to be related to the kingdoms of this world. At first this was not a serious problem for the early Christians. The Roman Empire provided the context within which they proclaimed their faith and in which Saint Paul undertook his missionary journeys, establishing churches in different parts of the Mediterranean region. Moreover, the hope still persisted that there would yet be a dramatic intervention by God which would make his kingdom manifest to all people. Therefore, what happened to the kingdoms of this world was irrelevant; they would pass away in the ultimate divine triumph. Their only significance was in providing the context within which the gospel could be proclaimed. This is made clear by Saint Paul in his letter to the Romans, where he advised his readers to respect the governing authorities as divinely appointed agents for preserving the peace (13:1-7).

The incidence of persecution began to change all that; the Roman authorities would not leave the Christians of the first century alone to get on with their missionary expansion. Hence they were forced into ghettos, and over the course of time this led some to withdraw from ordinary life in the world into monastic communities where the Faith could be preserved. This way of relating to society has continued throughout the ages and is expressed most commonly today in the West by the privatizing of religion and the marginalization of the church. If Christians are no longer persecuted in most countries, they are left alone to get on with their ecclesiastical affairs. This is benevolently tolerated as their option, a choice that has nothing to do with the ordering of society at large. And there are many Christians who have not only acquiesced in this secular dismissal of the relevance of Christianity to society as a whole but have positively embraced it as the way of preserving the integrity of the Faith uncontaminated by the standards of secularism.

This separation of the kingdoms cannot be sustained if Jesus established the reign of God over all people and the whole earth. In any case, the two kingdoms overlap: those who are citizens of the kingdom of God are at the same time citizens of earthly kingdoms, and the issue is how to live with this tension and how the divine kingdom is creatively to influence earthly citizenship. The attempt to resolve the dilemma by having the church take over the role of the state manifestly led to disastrous consequences. The church assumed this role when the emperor Constantine was converted to Christianity and declared it to be the official religion of the state. That led to the fatal compromise of the gospel of the kingdom, which occurred when the church accepted the world's terms for the exercise of divine sovereignty. That this was a fatal error was underlined again and again by successive popes arrogating political power to themselves, by Calvin's short-lived attempt to establish a theocratic government in

Geneva, and by the Tudor doctrine of the divine right of kings. Dante's condemnation of the papacy in his own day stands as a classical warning of what can happen when the proper distinction between the two realms is forgotten: "Rome, that made the good world, was wont to have two suns, which made plain to sight the one road and the other; that of the world and that of God. One hath quenched the other, and the sword is joined to the crook; and the one together with the other must perforce go ill, because, being joined, one feareth not the other."[2] The same danger is present whenever the church becomes established by the state. The tension between the two is subtly resolved, and the church may all too easily become the tool of the secular authority.

The other solution that has also proved to be profoundly unsatisfactory has been the doctrine of the two spheres rigidly separated from one another. This was made quite explicit in a letter that Hosius of Cordova addressed to the emperor Constantine at a time of acute theological controversy in which he sought to intervene: "Intrude not yourself into ecclesiastical matters, neither give commands unto us concerning them; but learn them from us. God has put into your hands the kingdom; to us he has entrusted the affairs of his church; and as he who would steal the empire from you would resist the ordinance of God, so likewise fear on your part lest by taking upon yourself the government of the Church, you become guilty of a great offence. It is written, 'Render unto Caesar the things that are Caesar's and unto God the things that are God's.' Neither therefore is it permitted unto us to exercise earthly rule, nor have you, Sire, any authority to burn incense."[3]

A somewhat more ambiguous version of the same thesis was expounded by Saint Augustine in the fifth century in *The City of*

2. Dante, quoted by Cyril Garbett in *Church and State in England* (Hodder & Stoughton, 1950), p. 17.
3. Athanasius, *Hist. Arian.* 44.

God. Following the fall of Rome to Alaric and his barbarian hordes, the cry was raised that the calamity was due to the forsaking of the ancient gods upon whom the protection of the city and the Empire had always depended; the adoption of Christianity after the accession of Constantine had been an unmitigated disaster for Rome. Such was the pagan argument that Augustine set himself to answer.

He describes his purpose as the defense of "the glorious City of God against those who prefer their own gods to its Founder," contrasting it with the earthly city, "which lusts to dominate the world and which, though nations bend to its yoke, is itself dominated by its passion for dominion."[4] Throughout the whole of the twenty-two books, Augustine makes it plain that he does not regard the earthly city, organized by man for his own ends, as having any enduring value. In fact, strictly speaking, it is not a city at all. For if Cicero is right in claiming that the state can only properly be described as existing when it is founded on justice (2.21), then the state has never truly existed in pagan society, because justice is possible only when the true God is given his due, and that only happens in the city of God (19.21).

The title of his work really summarizes the position that Augustine adopts: he does not call it "The Two Cities," because the earthly city interests him only by contrast with the city of God, the community of the faithful, which endures to eternity and alone gives life on earth any meaning. He even goes so far as to discount the significance of different forms of government: "When it is considered," he writes, "how short is the span of human life, does it really matter to a man whose days are numbered what government he must obey, so long as he is not compelled to act against God or his conscience?" (5.17). True, under earthly conditions, the history

4. Augustine, *The City of God*, Book 1, Preface. This and subsequent references to this source are taken from the English translation of Fathers of the Church by Demetrius B. Zema and Gerald G. Walsh (Doubleday, 1950).

of the two cities is inextricably intermingled (11.1), but it is only the city of God that has positive value. At best the earthly city is a necessary evil, and the peace it establishes is provisional. "The heavenly city, meanwhile — or, rather, that part that is on pilgrimage in mortal life and lives by faith — must use this earthly peace until such time as our mortality which needs such peace has passed away" (19.17). The earthly city is founded to counter man's sin (19.15) and is thus negative in purpose. No lasting happiness is to be found in it (19.5-7), although the Christian who is subject to earthly rulers may enjoy such happiness even in his subjection because of his citizenship in the city of God (19.13).

The broad conclusion of Augustine's argument would therefore appear to be otherworldly in character: the earthly city and its organization is of no lasting importance, and Christians should be concerned with that eternal city whose builder and maker is God. Yet the matter is not quite so simple. Augustine would have believers take their civic responsibilities seriously, and he even argues that the salvation of the Roman Empire ultimately turns on the Christian virtue of its citizens. In a letter to Marcellinus he replies to those who say that the teaching of Christ is opposed to the welfare of the state by bidding them "produce such provincial administrators, such husbands, such wives, such parents, such sons, such masters, such slaves, such kings, such judges, and finally such tax-payers and collectors of public revenue as Christian teaching requires them to be, and then let them dare to say that this teaching is opposed to the welfare of the state, or, rather, let them even hesitate to admit that it is the greatest safety of the state, if it is observed."[5] The earthly city could approximate to the shadow of the heavenly city, but in the end it is provisional and therefore must never be absolutized.

5. Augustine, *Ep.* 138, ET in Fathers of the Church by Parsons (Doubleday, 1953), p. 48.

Augustine stated the problem of church-state relations rather than solved it, and it proved all too easy for those who came afterward to get rid of the tension between church and state either by identifying the one with the other or by developing the doctrine of the two spheres, as Luther did, enjoining a strict separation between them. He described them as the left and right hands of God, neither entitled to interfere with the other, much as Hosius of Cordova had maintained in his letter to the emperor Constantine. It has frequently been pointed out that many of the troubles in Europe over the past four hundred years are traceable to the baneful effect of Luther's teaching on the relationship of church and state; for where it has been predominant, it has resulted in the abdication of Christian witness from any leadership in the field of social and international affairs. The state has been allowed to go to the devil if it would, because in the nature of the case the church had no guidance to give, no rightful influence to exert. Thus in the 1930s Nazism came to power in Germany in the moral and political vacuum for which otherworldly, privatized religion was in no small measure accountable. On the other hand, we must not forget that when the totalitarianism of the Hitler regime became apparent and the so-called German Christians became a tool in the hands of the Nazi leadership, the confessional movement came to birth within the Lutheran Church, leading to the now-famous Barmen Declaration, echoing the words of the apostle, "We ought to obey God rather than men."[6] Any attempt to minimize or avoid the tension between church and state will not do. Since the members of the church are also citizens of the state and the state itself is held to be a divine ordinance, no strict separation between the two spheres is defensible. The values of the kingdom of God will always be in tension with the practice of politics, though we should look for that tension to be as creative as possible.

6. Cf. Karl Barth, *Church Dogmatics* (T. & T. Clark, 1957), II.1, pp. 172-78.

The kingdom of God is not of this world. It stands in perpetual judgment of it as the reality that confounds all human pretensions. How that tension is to be maintained and witness borne to the reality of God's reign when Christians are inextricably bound up with living in a world which is alienated from God will be the subject of the chapters that follow. Christians live in what has been called the overlap of the ages, and that inevitably causes tension and, not infrequently, conflict.

CHAPTER SEVEN

The Challenge
of the Kingdom

If the kingdom of God on earth was effectively established by the life, death, and resurrection of Jesus, this became a reality for all time, not simply for the first century to which the New Testament bears witness. One thing is patently clear. The kingdom did not replace the historical order, as many at first expected it would do. The world went on much as before. The kingdom supervened on the old order, and until the end of time Christians were called upon to live in two kingdoms in constant tension with one another: the kingdom of God and the kingdoms of this world. The consummation of God's reign awaits the end of history, however long or short a period of time that will be. But for Christians the Lordship of Christ is both the assurance and the earnest of God's ultimate and manifest sovereignty over all things. This came to be affirmed without equivocation by the time that the Fourth Gospel was written.

In recent years some New Testament scholars have made much of the difficulty, if not impossibility, of spanning the centuries between the culture, the thought forms, and the plausibility structures of the ancient world and those of the modern West, with its knowledge, scientific achievements, and technological expertise. Of course the differences are very great. But I believe they have been far too uncritically exaggerated. One of the most obvious and fundamental differences is that in the ancient world belief in God or supernatural beings was taken for granted. Human beings were thought of not as masters of their environment but as subjects of higher powers. Since the Enlightenment, the growth of secularism has taken over the public realm, and Swinburne's famous lines "Glory to man in the highest; for man is the master of things" have become the context within which industrialized society has been allowed to develop. If that is assumed to be how things really are, then any talk of the kingdom must be held to be irrelevant to the modern scene, and decisions on public policy are rightly made without reference to the will and purpose of God. But why should that assumption be accepted, especially at a time when Western culture is in a state of confusion and is manifestly disintegrating? Why should those who continue to believe that God is the Creator and Lord of the universe be expected to make their religious beliefs conform to and cohere with a basic assumption which they see every reason to reject? Instead of trying to accommodate to a plausibility structure that they believe to be transitory and fundamentally flawed, they are bound to engage in a radical critique of the prevailing modern assumptions and all that follows from them.

This has been the theme of the series of recent publications under the rubric "The Gospel and Our Culture," initiated by the British Council of Churches (now replaced by the Council of Churches for Britain and Ireland) under the chairmanship of Bishop Hugh Montefiore. The series arose in response to the writings of Bishop Lesslie Newbigin, in particular to his *The Other Side of 1984*.[1] His thesis is that we have come to the breakdown and end of the Enlightenment and that we have to take seriously the biblical worldview as a profound challenge to Western culture. Newbigin not only believes that this is a serious and radical challenge but that it summons the churches to engage in a mission to modern culture,

1. Newbigin, *The Other Side of 1984* (World Council of Churches, 1983).

and that means entering again into the public sphere. No longer can Christians be content with privatized religion. They have to claim the sovereignty of God over the whole of life, over international and social relationships as much as over individual behavior. Christianity cannot be confined to a private realm of personal morals, as many would like it to be. It is concerned with the public realm, with the values that inform the ordering of society and the way these are expressed in practice.

Acceptance of this thesis implies asking in what ways the kingdom of God challenges and is in tension with secular assumptions and practices. Basic to this is a radical revolution in the concept of sovereignty. Most people assume that it is the exercise of political power understood as the right to govern by force, either by tyranny or by democratic mandate. To equate sovereignty with political power so understood is to create an intractable human dilemma, for it entails the assumption that political power carries with it absolute authority, which it manifestly does not. Stalin believed that it did, arrogantly responding to the pope's moral condemnation of his tyrannical dictatorship with the sarcastic comment "How many divisions does he command?"

When tyranny is arbitrarily exercised, it loses all moral authority. It provokes rebellion and has within it the seeds of its own disintegration. This was made clear by the collapse of the Soviet Union and the discrediting of the Communist system. But the same dilemma is inherent in democratic government. It too provokes conflict when minorities find themselves in opposition to the elected majority; the government of the day may soon lose moral authority when it is tempted to ride roughshod over its opponents. Democracy may be the best form of government available to us, but too much should not be claimed for it, for it has not solved the problem of relating sovereignty to authority. It is a healthy corrective to pretentious claims to be reminded of Plato's classification of forms of government in *The Republic* as long ago as the fifth century B.C.

Plato placed them in a potentially degenerating order, beginning with aristocracy as the rule of the best people. After that came timocracy — the rule of the ambitious; then oligarchy — the rule of the few; then democracy; and finally tyranny.[2] His low estimate of democracy, which he believed could easily degenerate into tyranny, was based on his experience in fifth-century Athens, where he had seen how the assembly of the people could be influenced and carried away by any plausible demagogue. This has a strangely modern ring to it. We have only to think of the way in which Hitler mesmerized a whole nation.

As we look around the modern world, we are bound to be struck by the prevalence of dictatorships, all of them oppressive and some blatantly tyrannical, and we can see, as in the recent case of Saddam Hussein, how, given the power of monopolized propaganda, they can be supported by popular enthusiasm. The development of parliamentary democracy has gone some way to counter autocratic rule. The American constitution, with its built-in division and balance of powers between the executive in the White House and the Congress on Capitol Hill, is a case in point. But the American presidency, with its enormous powers which were so scandalously misused by Richard Nixon in the Watergate affair, does not commend itself as the obvious model that other nations should adopt. Further, the authority of the president and of members of Congress depends on elections held every few years, and the mandate this gives them not only when they are elected but more so in the intervening period bristles with problems.

In the United Kingdom, which, unlike America, has no written constitution, the relationship between authority and political power has become a subject of considerable controversy. For many years the British have had a government elected by only a minority vote. Moreover, the discipline exercised by party whips and the diminution

2. Plato, *The Republic*, Books 8 and 9.

of influence on the part of backbenchers lay behind Lord Hailsham's Dimbleby lecture on the BBC in the 1980s, in which he argued that we had reached the situation where we now had an elected dictatorship. With the coming to power in April 1992 of a fourth minority Conservative government that commanded far less than half the votes of the electorate, the question of constitutional reform is bound to be in the forefront of the political agenda. We are already beginning to see a strong campaign mounted for the devolution of government to the regions and local authorities, and the case for proportional representation will be increasingly hard to resist. But whatever changes are made, the problem of authority will not be solved. Proportional representation would be an important step forward in providing government that was responsible to a majority rather than a minority of electors, but majorities do not necessarily carry moral authority, as Plato saw so clearly. Their policies may be contrary to the public welfare, and they may justifiably provoke opposition and rebellion. Minorities may sometimes have what is morally right on their side. Every government, whatever its composition or method of appointment, has at best limited authority.

Therefore, we have to recognize that a distinction needs to be drawn between political power and moral authority. This is partially illustrated by the institution of the British monarchy, which has proved to be a stabilizing influence in public life. Its strength lies in any authority it has being separated from the exercise of political power, and it has been suggested that this offers a safeguard against any government in Britain arrogating to itself absolute power and authority. The authority of the monarchy lies in its being a focus of loyalty based on its setting a high standard of public service. Of course, this has not always been so. In the Tudor and Stuart periods, absolute authority and political power were combined in the monarchy, which was undergirded by the doctrine of the divine right of kings. But to return to that is inconceivable in the modern world. As long as the Crown remains firmly divorced from the exercise of political power and is seen as setting standards for public life, there is little chance of abolitionists persuading the British people to adopt some form of republicanism. In practice, the alternative appears to open the door still wider to autocracy and the abuse of power by which republican constitutions seem to be bedeviled. However, too much should not be claimed for the monarchy. It is at best a precarious corrective to absolutist political pretensions and depends for its acceptability on the readiness of the heirs to the throne to adapt sensitively and imaginatively to changing social conditions.

The authority of government is not alone in being questioned. Today there is a widespread rejection of authority of all kinds, whether it be of parents, schoolteachers, officers of the law, or anyone who presumes to tell others what they ought to do. This is rooted in the presumption of freedom to do just what one likes. The poet Henley's famous words "I am the master of my fate; I am the captain of my soul" have become for many people the only standard by which to live. But when all moral authority is disregarded, society disintegrates, and the law of the jungle prevails, though that description is hardly fair to the animals! In the face of this, it is surely necessary to maintain that there is only one absolute and self-authenticating moral authority, and that is God. His reign is then seen as expressed in the moral authority with which he rules the world. That is an authority which no human being or institution can command and which stands in judgment over all human pretensions to power.

That is how we may begin to understand the challenge of the kingdom of God to the kingdoms of this world. It is clarified by tracing the development of the idea of the kingdom as the reign of God in the pages of the Bible. The Old Testament gives two different accounts of what happened when the people in ancient Israel demanded that a king should be anointed to rule over them. In the first, Samuel's reaction to the demand was one of displeasure because he felt that the people were challenging his authority. So he prayed for guidance about what he should do. The answer he got was

"Listen to the people and all that they are saying; they have not rejected you, it is I whom they have rejected, I whom they will not have to be their king. . . . Hear what they have to say now, but give them a solemn warning and tell them what sort of king will govern them" (1 Sam. 8:7, 9). The second account has a slightly different emphasis. Samuel summoned the people to meet him at Mizpah and told them that in spite of their rejection of the God who had delivered them from bondage in Egypt and from all the kingdoms that had oppressed them, he had been authorized to make arrangements for the choice of someone to rule over them (1 Sam. 10:17-19). What is common to both accounts is the assertion that Yahweh, the God of Israel, is the only true king. If they insisted on appointing one of their number to assume office, they must take the consequences. So the lot fell on Saul.

By the time David had succeeded him, kingship had come to be established, but it was redefined in terms of a solemn covenant between Yahweh and the house of David. It was acknowledged that the only true king was Yahweh himself and that all ultimate authority was vested in him. Israel's earthly king was simply his representative charged with ruling the kingdom in accordance with the divine will and with establishing the nation in righteousness, justice, and peace. That David recognized his full responsibility to Yahweh is confirmed by the outcome of the story of Bathsheba. After the king had fallen in love with her and made her pregnant, he had arranged for her husband, Uriah, to be in the forefront of battle against the Ammonites, where he was killed. David then took Bathsheba to be his wife. When Nathan the prophet in the name of the Lord challenged David with what he had done, he made no excuse, nor did he claim that he could do what he liked, but admitted, "I have sinned against the Lord" (2 Sam. 12:13). He acknowledged that he had betrayed the covenant to which he was committed and which was the basis of his kingship. Yahweh was the true king of Israel and indeed the king of all the nations. His sovereignty was supreme, and every earthly ruler was subject to his judgment. David owed his authority solely to him. That was the theme of many psalms composed for the worship of the temple at Jerusalem, psalms that celebrated the kingship of Yahweh over the whole earth.[3]

It is, therefore, not surprising that when Jesus came on the scene announcing the imminent coming of the kingdom of God and claiming to be God's authorized representative in bringing it to pass, questions should be asked about his role. Who was this claiming divine authority? Was he not virtually claiming to be king of the Jews? This must surely have been one of the reasons, perhaps the decisive reason, for Pilate's handing Jesus over to be crucified. There has been a great deal of debate about why the crucifixion took place and who was ultimately responsible. But there is no reasonable doubt that the Roman procurator caused the superscription "The King of the Jews" to be fixed to the cross, and the account of the trial of Jesus before Pilate in the Fourth Gospel in which the question of kingship was raised may well reflect what actually happened. Whether or not Pilate believed that Jesus was a real threat to Roman authority, there were enough signs of discontent and possible insurgence for the procurator to think that the inscription on the cross would serve as a salutory warning to possible troublemakers.

But there is no evidence to suggest that Jesus made any pretension to political power. He appears to have accepted the framework of government in Palestine. For example, whatever we make of the cryptic answer to the trick question about whether or not tribute should be paid to Caesar, it appears that Jesus took Roman rule for granted and did not believe that his role was to challenge it. Nor did he make any claim to kingship in the Davidic sense. But his announcement of the coming of the kingdom of God and his claim

3. Cf. Aubrey R. Johnson, *The Sacral Kingship in Ancient Israel* (University of Wales Press, 1955).

to his own absolute authority must have suggested to some people that he had pretensions to some sort of kingship. Misconceptions easily arise and attract wide currency when superficial judgments are made about anybody's intentions.

One of the most striking things about the ministry of Jesus was that he renounced power as that was commonly understood and at the same time claimed divine authority. "He taught them as one that had authority, and not as the scribes" (Mark 1:22, KJV), and this is reflected in the so-called Great Commission that Matthew attributes to Jesus: "Full authority in heaven and on earth has been committed to me" (Matt. 28:18). For the overwhelming majority of people, authority entails the exercise of power understood as enforcement. The disciples of Jesus were as bewildered as anyone else at the refusal of their Master to equate the two and to submit to suffering and death as the way of establishing his authority. For those who believe that nothing is achieved in this world except by compulsion, by forcing other people to submit to their will, the idea that moral authority is more powerful than physical or manipulative force seems wholly unrealistic, if not incomprehensible. But the primitive church had to begin to come to terms with the paradox. Early Christians were helped to do so by their belief in the resurrection. But this did not alter the fact that Jesus had died an ignominious death at the hands of those who continued to wield power. If they were now to acknowledge him as Lord — almost certainly the earliest confession of Christian faith and a denial of the Roman emperor's claim to absolute lordship and authority — they had to start to come to terms with the way in which he exercised authority. And that meant taking the crucifixion seriously. Did it establish a moral authority against which no exercise of political power could ultimately prevail?

That was Paul's conviction, startlingly declared in his first letter to the Corinthian church: "This doctrine of the cross is sheer folly to those on their way to ruin, but to us who are on the way to salvation it is the power of God. . . . We proclaim Christ — yes,

Christ nailed to the cross; and though this is a stumbling-block to Jews and folly to Greeks, yet to those who have heard his call, Jews and Greeks alike, he is the power of God and the wisdom of God" (1 Cor. 1:18, 23-24). Omnipotence displayed on a Roman cross! That is to turn upside down all human understanding of and pretension to power. We inevitably start with our human definitions of power to which we and all previous generations have been conditioned and which we have taken for granted. The shock of having to come to terms with a concept of power so radically different is considerable. But, as Karl Barth once maintained, if we believe in God, we must not start with our own limited concepts and make them the touchstone of how things actually are; we must bring them under the judgment of divine revelation.[4]

What then are we to say about divine providence, and what sense are we to make of claiming that God reigns and is the Lord of history and the whole universe? If we start with the gospel of the kingdom as proclaimed and acted out by Jesus, we are driven to the conclusion that God does not do what we expect him to do. He does not intervene in human affairs or indeed in the world of nature as we would do if we were omnipotent and exercised power in the way in which we understand it. The fact is that God, if he does exist and is the Lord of history, does not override human freedom or indeed the freedom of the natural order. That does not explain the mystery of evil. It only underlines the words of the prophet of old: "For my thoughts are not your thoughts, and your ways are not my ways. . . . For as the heavens are higher than the earth, so are my ways higher than your ways and my thoughts than your thoughts" (Isa. 55:8-9).

This does not entail the eighteenth-century Deist view that God had abandoned his creation and left it to its own devices. On the contrary, the gospel of the kingdom is about God's involvement at

---

4. See Barth, *The Knowledge of God and the Service of God* (Hodder & Stoughton, 1938), p. 33.

every point, sharing in and bearing the world's suffering. We are not alone in carrying the burden of freedom. It is God's burden far more than ours, and that is the message of the cross.

One of the curious things about John Bowden's book entitled *Jesus: The Unanswered Questions* is his failure to come to grips with the problem of the nature of power and what the New Testament has to say about it; and this despite his insistence that the eighth chapter of his book, called "Jesus, Power and Politics," contains the central thrust of his argument, which he complains David Edwards has largely ignored in his criticism. But the chapter is mainly concerned with the manipulation of power, particularly in the church. What he has to say about this is often very much to the point, for the manipulation of people and ideas is an insidious way in which power is widely exercised. But the basic question is what constitutes real power. Only when we have answered this question can we fruitfully discuss how it should be exercised. That is a question of the utmost urgency in a world where popular understandings of power and how it should be exercised have brought us to the brink of catastrophe and the possible annihilation of the human race.

The crux of the matter comes to a head in the threat of war, in the incidence of violence all over the world, of which war is the ultimate expression, filling the television screen and the pages of our daily newspapers. The most that the majority of people hope for is that it can be contained, if only temporarily. Few believe it can be challenged. In wrestling with the problem, the church devised and developed the doctrine of the just war, which was held to be the only way of living with the inevitability of conflict and controlling it by moral principles. But this doctrine has become more and more difficult to sustain and defend during this century. Two world wars and their often violent aftermath, with the invention and stockpiling of terrible instruments of mass destruction, have made the moral arguments in the traditional doctrine increasingly hard to advance. The theory of deterrence has not helped very much, for to threaten to use nuclear weapons makes no sense unless you are prepared to use them should the threat fail to deter.

The question that must now be seriously considered is whether going to war is any longer justifiable on either moral or practical grounds. Failure to use armed force to oppose aggression and resort to passive resistance would undoubtedly result in widespread suffering and the loss of cherished liberties by many people. But this has to be weighed against the carnage and devastation that a modern war inevitably causes, not to mention the brutality and violence that would be engendered in the victors, if there were any. Violence breeds violence, as we have seen all too clearly in recent years. On the other hand, dictatorship has within it the seeds of its own self-destruction. History shows us that while a dictator may survive for a long time, in the end his hold over the population he oppresses weakens to the point where it can no longer be sustained. It is too early yet to assess the full implications of the collapse of the Soviet empire from within, but the belief of many in the West — that after Stalin the expansion and world domination of the Communist system could be contained and prevented only by a global war involving mass devastation and destruction — has proved to be wrong. While most people would still not be prepared even to entertain the question I have asked, on sheer practical grounds of common sense it has to be considered and debated.

The immediate response to such an argument would certainly be an appeal to moral principles. Weighing the practical cost of armed opposition to aggression and dictatorship against the suffering, oppression, and loss of liberty that would result from passive and moral resistance would be held to flout the moral values we are called upon to defend, and freedom would be invoked as something that we cannot surrender without ceasing to be responsible human beings. But freedom for whom? Not for the casualties of war. Only potentially for those who survive, and what will they do with whatever comes out of the holocaust? Freedom is an ambiguous word, and it is a dangerously emotional one when it is used simplistically as a standard for going into battle. Freedom to do what you want provided you can get away with it is not an absolute value. Without responsibility it is of no value, and what is claimed for it in propaganda is often a cover for something much less defensible. In the recent confrontation with President Saddam Hussein, the reason given for the justifiability of engaging in armed conflict was his aggression and occupation of Kuwait. What was muted was the question of the control of oil supplies in the Gulf and the consequent economic problems that this would cause the Western nations in particular. Behind this, other issues were at stake, such as the rise of Arab nationalism and its opposition to economic imperialism, which seemed to many evidenced by the arrival of massive American forces in Saudi Arabia. The issues behind a conflict are much more complex than can be contained in a moral slogan. Moreover, there are the complications caused by the international arms trade, which has produced great wealth for many people and without which large-scale conflict in the Middle East would not have been possible.

The confusion about the exercise of power in the face of the threat of war is but a reflection of the problem endemic in every human society. When "there was no king in Israel and every man did what was right in his own eyes" (Judg. 17:6), no ordered society was possible. And without acknowledged moral authority today, anarchy and disintegration are bound to follow. Human government is increasingly felt to lack this authority. That is where the authority of God which alone can claim to be absolute and the kingdom of which he alone is sovereign become strikingly relevant to the problems we face. But if this is taken seriously, we have to recognize that God does not exercise his authority by intervening to compel people to do what is right, nor does he manipulate them to achieve his own purposes. The model for his providence is the ministry of Jesus and his death and resurrection.

This has been taken seriously by many Christians. For example, the Society of Friends has maintained a powerful witness to the effectiveness of nonviolence and the moral authority of God expressed in love for every man, woman, and child whose ultimate value is to be respected and not overridden by any manipulation, human or divine. Its Committee of Sufferings, which is the umbrella for the concerns of Friends in social and international affairs, may sound strangely titled to most people. But it significantly expresses the way in which members of the Society approach contemporary problems. Nobody who knows anything about their activity and involvement could accuse them of lacking realism or avoiding harsh analysis or withdrawing from engagement in the practical problems of society. Many in the mainstream churches have followed the same line, such as those who were conscientious objectors on Christian grounds in both world wars, and notable public figures and prominent churchmen like Charles Raven, Donald Soper, and George Macleod. They cannot be dismissed as naive eccentrics.

A complex of domestic problems remains centered on the enforcement of law and the unsatisfactory state of our penal system. It is worth noting that where capital punishment has been abolished, it is a sign of changing perspectives on how human beings should be treated. For centuries it was taken for granted that capital punishment was the only way of dealing with serious and sometimes trivial offenders. All that has changed. The sacredness of human life and the moral imperative to respect it have overridden considerations of political expediency. At all events, the time has surely come to take seriously those who have insisted on the distinction between moral authority and the manipulation of political power. The power of coercion divorced from moral authority is destructive of human society. The power of moral authority that renounces coercion is constructive. In a sinful world, an element of coercion seems to be unavoidable. But the gospel of the kingdom requires us to minimize it as far as we can and give far more weight than we do to the powers of persuasion, the moral critique of the manipulation of people and ideas, and the ultimate triumph of goodness when it is seen expressed in self-sacrifice for others and service for the common good.

The problems of putting this into practice seem overwhelming in a world where evil is rampant, but the gospel of the kingdom challenges us to think again and not to be satisfied with the easy and what appear to be the obvious answers. If God reigns and exercises his sovereignty in ways that conflict with our assumptions, are not those assumptions called into question? Have we any grounds for hope unless we acknowledge the power of his ultimate authority? This is a totally different kind of sovereignty and power from that of the kingdoms of this world and is in constant tension with them. Yet if Jesus died and rose again for the whole human race, that is the reality which underlies human existence. It relativizes all human claims to sovereignty and must ultimately prevail.

CHAPTER EIGHT

Inevitable Tensions

Given that the kingdom of God was established by the advent, life, teaching, death, and resurrection of Jesus, Christians are bound to experience tension in relating to a secular and pluralist society. However, they may sometimes find themselves advocating principles that are shared by humanists or those who make a different religious profession. The widest possible consensus is to be welcomed, because this offers the hope of more effective influence. At other points the distinctiveness of the gospel of the kingdom will run counter to many common assumptions. Christians have no warrant to impose the values of the kingdom on a pluralist society, but if those values are enshrined in the nature of things and the proclamation of the kingdom is a declaration of what is in fact the case, there is an inescapable obligation to make that plain.

In the first place, the universalist nature of the kingdom is a profound challenge to the exclusivist and discriminatory characteristics of modern secular society. We have already seen that Jesus, following the universalist proclamations of the sovereignty of God over the whole world in the second part of the prophecy of Isaiah and its reiteration in the Psalms, challenged the exclusiveness of the Pharisees in his day by declaring that everyone in Israel, whoever they might be, could enter the kingdom provided they repented and put their trust in him. He also extended this offer to those who were not Israelites, thus laying the foundation for the invitation to Gentiles that carried the day at the Council of Jerusalem (recorded in Acts 15), against those who still believed that Gentiles had to become Jews before they could be accepted into the Christian community. This led to Saint Paul's missionary journeys and the proclamation of the gospel to the whole world.

The kingdom of God is therefore open to everyone irrespective of nation, race, color, sex, or class. In the words of Saint Paul in his letter to the Galatians, "Through faith you are all sons of God in union with Christ Jesus. Baptized into union with him, you have all put on Christ as a garment. There is no such thing as Jew and Greek, slave and freeman, male and female; for you are all one person in Christ Jesus" (3:26-29). The worldwide church, despite its sectarian divisions, is an abiding witness to the universalist nature of the kingdom, which stands as a perpetual challenge to every form of exclusivism or discrimination, whether in the church itself or in society at large.

Second, in the light of the current treatment of our environment and the exploitation of our natural resources, we are called upon to reaffirm that the whole world belongs to God and is under his jurisdiction. As the Psalmist proclaimed, "The earth is the Lord's and all that is in it, the world and those who dwell therein" (24:1). We are not free to do what we like with it. We are not entitled to exploit it, but we are called upon to act as stewards responsible to God for the way we treat it. Environmental issues have in recent years come to the top of the political agenda, but they are generally presented in terms of our responsibilities to future generations and the danger to ourselves from pollution and exhaustion of natural resources through wanton industrial exploitation to achieve quick profits. This is certainly true, and Christians are on common ground with secular humanists in insisting that action should be taken immediately to reverse destructive and potentially catastrophic trends. But the biblical challenge goes much further. We are fundamentally responsible to God, and it is in reference to him that there is the strongest grounding for the radical changes of attitude that are required. The perils we face have their roots in the glorification of man and his ability to manage his own affairs, which Swinburne celebrated without reference to any higher authority.

Third, and closely connected to the warnings against exploitation of the environment, is the condemnation of greed and the rejection of the accumulation of material possessions as the obvious goal of human endeavor. There can be no doubt that both have become firmly entrenched in Western society, and sensitive nerves begin to be touched when these issues are subjected to any criticism. Unlimited economic growth has come to be taken for granted as a clearly desirable objective, and the value of individuals is widely assessed by the amount of money at their disposal. "What is he worth?" expects the answer "So many pounds or dollars." It is obvious that this comes into conflict with the many warnings of Jesus about the perils of the pursuit of riches, summarized by the words in 1 Timothy: "the love of money is the root of all evil" (6:10).

Of course, this can be pressed too far. David L. Edwards in his recent book about the future of Europe is surely right in arguing that there has been a danger in some quarters of downgrading from a Christian point of view the value of the production of wealth.[1] Without economic growth, the needs of the growing world population cannot be met. A prosperous Europe would be of great benefit not only to its own peoples but also to the underdeveloped and developing world. But the underlying question is what wealth really is. Is it to be measured in terms of the quantity or the quality of the products of modern technology? How far do they contribute to the creation of poverty? What are the human values that underlie

1. Edwards, *Christians in a New Europe* (Collins–Fount Paperbacks, 1990), pp. 26-28.

the whole economic enterprise? In attempting to answer these questions, the values of the kingdom begin to be seen as in acute tension, if not open conflict, with purely materialistic answers and the practices that follow from them.

The major difficulty in answering these questions is the confusing smoke screen that the paper economy casts over the real economy. The paper economy is calculated in terms of money, which is conveniently quantifiable. But money has no value in itself; it is simply the symbol for the real economy — for land, machinery, products, artifacts, and services on which a price is placed according to the vagaries of the market. However, in assessing their true value, money is a very clumsy tool; for value cannot be measured quantitatively without distortion and the overlooking of questions of quality. Moreover, there is much of the real economy that lies outside the market and to which price fixing is not applied.

The most obvious example of this is the domestic economy — the management of homes and the care of families — and to it should be added the widespread forms of voluntary activity that contribute so much to the welfare of society. All this falls outside the calculations of the gross national product, and in so doing makes monetary computations misleading. Moreover, the market economy itself is not in practice limited to the fixing of price mechanisms. Governments do in fact have to intervene by introducing values that do not lend themselves to numerical assessment. If the money market is left to itself, the social consequences are completely unacceptable: some become increasingly rich in monetary terms, with the overwhelming power and influence that this entails, while large numbers of people are deprived of any decent livelihood. This has to be mitigated by state action whatever the political and economic aims of the privileged few. Much of state expenditure — for instance, on health and social services and on the environment — is due to the recognition that the market to a very large extent ignores the quality of life and has to be corrected and controlled by values that do not lend themselves to purely quantitative calculations. The great political debate is really about this. To what extent should the free operations of the market be encouraged to produce the goods and services that people need, and to what extent should the government intervene to ensure that the quality of life is enhanced for all? The American economist Kenneth Galbraith explored this issue when he spoke of the dangers of the spread of private affluence alongside public squalor.

If, therefore, wealth is to be properly assessed, we have to get behind the smoke screen of the money market and ask what the real values are that we should seek to promote. And that is where the challenge of the kingdom of God becomes extremely relevant and leads to some very disturbing questions. If we examine the criterion of growth as defined by the increase of the gross national product, arbitrarily defined by what can be quantified and numerically computed, we realize that there is a great deal of production that contributes not to the wealth of nations like Great Britain and the United States but to their impoverishment. If the quality of life is the touchstone of wealth, we are bound to raise questions about the massive arms trade, the industries that pollute the environment, and the manufacture of vast quantities of throwaway products. For example, how in terms of real wealth, real value, are we to defend the growth of the automobile industry, which fills our roads with more and more cars and trucks, clogs the streets of our cities to the point where traffic is unable to move, causes death and injury on a frightening scale, forces through the spoliation of the countryside by a massive road-building program, and pollutes the atmosphere with carbon-monoxide emissions? The invention of the internal combustion engine has provided mobility for increasing numbers of people, though that is showing increasingly diminishing returns. But the question of the proportionate value of this to the mounting consequences listed above has now to be taken seriously, whatever the resistance of the vested interests of the automotive organizations, the manufacturers, and the trade unions. The practical steps that will have to be taken are bound to be controversial, but they will have to be decided in the light of value judgments: where real wealth ultimately lies. Is the multiplication of the number of cars and trucks on the roads an increase in the wealth of the country, while the performance of successful operations in our hospitals lies outside the computation?

I have chosen this particular example to show that the values of the kingdom and the teaching of Jesus have direct, if controversial, bearing on practical questions about the way in which we regard the creation of wealth. They challenge the kind of assumptions that are widely and uncritically taken for granted about the maximizing of monetary profit, which cloaks a distortion of where wealth really lies.

Another way of directing attention to the confusion that arises when the making of money contradicts the creation of wealth is to urge the distinction between needs and wants. It is obvious that everyone needs certain things if they are to have a reasonable livelihood: food, clothing, a home, and means of enjoying leisure. The latter covers a multitude of things, which the free market is designed to supply. But it also creates wants that are stimulated by advertising agencies. The result is the creation of a voracious appetite for more and more useless possessions at the cost of the social provision of many things needed to enhance the welfare of the whole country and tackle the deprivation of a growing section of the community.

The values of the kingdom of God call for a change of attitude toward money and wealth that will obviously meet with fierce resistance. Valuing people according to the amount of money they have at their disposal should be replaced by the criterion of what they contribute to the welfare of their neighbors and the community at large. The accumulation of large financial fortunes should be regarded not as a proper measure of success but as a distortion of the health of society. No business executive is worth the huge salaries that have come to be paid or the golden handshakes followed by massive pensions, and the extravagant rewards given to sports figures, pop singers, and certain entrepreneurs make a mockery of justice when others have to scrape for a living. In addition, these fortunes concentrate far too much power in the hands of a few individuals. The continued toleration of these huge discrepancies cannot be defended; it involves a glorification of money and an incitement to greed that are a blot on civilized society and that parade values which can only be called obscene. Certainly they are in conflict with the ethics of the kingdom of God and the explicit warnings of Jesus.

Fourth, and closely allied to the criticism of the selfish pursuit of wealth, is the fundamental critique by the gospel of the kingdom of the individualism that has come to dominate much of people's thinking and attitude toward life in the Western world. The collapse of communism has inevitably been caused by and led to the demand for political and economic freedom that has so long been suppressed in many countries. But if this results in the insistence that everybody should do what they like and pursue their own interests as far as they possibly can, the end of the road is anarchy and the disintegration of society. Freedom conceived negatively as the removal of constraints is a recipe for social disaster. To reply that what is being positively advocated is that people should take responsibility for their own lives and that of their families without dependence on the state or public welfare, which is valid as far as it goes, ignores the fact that we are dependent on one another and that it is our relationship to one another which makes us what we are. The emphasis on human rights is undoubtedly of great importance, especially in the face of the widespread violation of human dignity that has been one of the most terrible features of the modern world. But rights divorced from responsibility are a wholly inadequate way of understanding how human beings should be regarded. Freedom that is not conceived as responsibility for one another is a seriously limited and distorted principle.

Clearly, the ethics of the kingdom have no place for unqualified individualism. On the contrary, they define human beings in terms of relationships, primarily to God and then to one another. This was vividly illustrated by Saint Paul in his metaphor of the body: "If one organ suffers, they all suffer together. If one flourishes, they all rejoice together. Now you are Christ's body, and each of you a limb or organ of it" (1 Cor. 12:26-27). What applies to the church applies to the whole human family. We belong together. We depend on one another. We are responsible to and for one another.

This means that concern for the poor, the homeless, the handicapped, and the underprivileged must be at the top of the Christian agenda. This is made abundantly plain when we remember the emphasis of Jesus in the announcement of his mission in the synagogue at Nazareth. Quoting Isaiah, he is reported to have declared, "The spirit of the Lord is upon me because he has anointed me; he has sent me to announce good news to the poor, to proclaim release for prisoners and recovery of sight for the blind; to let the broken victims go free, to proclaim the year of the Lord's favor" (Luke 4:18-19). These were not simply words; they were translated into action as Jesus consorted with the outcasts of the society of his time, much to the offense of the established authorities. When elections were called in Britain in 1992, corporate responsibility for the poor and deprived — what are called the underclass in our society — did not feature as priorities. Despite representations from the welfare and relief agencies concerned with the underprivileged, the homeless, and the outcasts, and even more with the millions of suffering and starving in the underdeveloped countries, all this seemed to be forgotten in the appeal to the private pocket and the need to cut income tax. From the standpoint of the kingdom, this is a glaring example of how far our values have become distorted and our priorities misplaced. And yet the majority of the population are generous at heart, as evidenced by the widespread response to appeals on television for victims of famine and natural disasters.

These are some of the values of the kingdom of God that are in tension if not in conflict with those of secular society. But they are not otherworldly. Jesus prayed not that his disciples should be taken out of the world but that they should be kept from the evil in it. Christians do have influence on both private morality and public policy, and in the chapters that follow we shall identify signs of the kingdom in what is still the overlap of the ages.

CHAPTER NINE

The Ambiguity
of the Church

Those who have followed the argument thus far may be prepared to concede that a case has been made for the kind of kingdom that Jesus proclaimed, and that it does challenge the kingdoms of this world. But the question remains whether the idea that God rules the world in this way is only a theory for which there is no evidence. Are there any unmistakable signs that he does so?

We can begin to answer this question by pointing to the continued existence of the Christian church throughout the centuries and now extending to every corner of the globe. Despite the ambiguity of this as a sign of the kingdom due to the repeated failure of the church in every age to live up to its high calling, nevertheless it is a fact that has to be taken seriously. Some years ago at a conference in Scotland, following a particularly scathing criticism of the church in the British Isles, one of those present was heard to remark, "I wonder what the Orthodox Church would make of that!" He was thinking of its glorious liturgy, which it has celebrated down the centuries and which has been the focus of faith and hope throughout seven decades of suppression and persecution in the Soviet Union and elsewhere. Karl Marx and those who followed him in establishing governments based on the power of the state believed that religion would prove to be an outdated fantasy and that the church would wither and die once the party had shown the way to the classless society. They have been manifestly shown to have been wrong. It is the church that has survived and in many cases has been the center of resistance to dictatorial regimes as well as the focus of new hope for the future.

Communist parties and governments have found to their bewilderment that the loyalties of people to Christianity and Islam have been far stronger and far more durable than their adherence to a political system, particularly when that system has proved to be autocratic and unable to deliver the promises of a better way of life and a better standard of living. The first clear sign of a breakdown was in Poland, where the Roman Catholic Church obviously had an almost universal hold on the hopes and loyalties of the people. But the same picture rapidly emerged in the countries of Eastern Europe, especially in the German Democratic Republic, where the churches became at first the focus of resistance and then a major catalyst in effecting change and moving toward a society in which freedom was respected. Even in China, where the church was thought to have virtually disappeared in the cultural revolution, it has emerged from underground with far greater strength than anyone could possibly have imagined; indeed, it is not hard to detect the signs of a future transformation of Chinese society, in which the submerged spiritual aspirations and needs of the people will come to the surface and the church will have a significant part to play in meeting them. The lesson of history, underlined by the recent dramatic events in Europe and elsewhere, is that the spiritual aspirations of people cannot be satisfied by those who promise material prosperity alone. The church, with all its blemishes and failure to be what it was intended to be, outlives and outlasts the kingdoms of this world, whose rulers and empires fade into obscurity. They are put into historical perspective by the example of Pilate, who would have been forgotten unless he had been responsible for crucifying Jesus. The survival and re-emergence of the church has to be taken seriously as a sign of the reality of the kingdom of God and the persistence of his providential activity in the world.

Christians would claim that this phenomenon is not attributable to mere human agency. It is guaranteed by the abiding presence and activity of the risen Christ. He alone preserves the continuity and indestructibility of the church. The church is not the kingdom; it is the witness to it. As Karl Barth rightly maintains, its essential function is to testify to the gospel, to the radical change in the human situation brought about by the crucifixion, resurrection, and ascension of Jesus. That and that alone gives it its authority, delegated to it insofar as it is faithful in proclamation, liturgy, and life. Its authority is not vested in its leaders or theologians, however prestigious they may be. The way in which they have been appointed, whether by apostolic succession or election, does not itself confer authority, though that has often been claimed, especially in the Catholic tradition. Their authority lies solely in their fidelity to the gospel. As I have said, the church is not the kingdom; it can only be a sign of it, a witness to it. And Jesus, the living head of the church, alone preserves its continuity and indestructibility. Were it merely a collection of sinful men and women, it would have perished in the tides of history. The fact that it persists, expands, and emerges again and again after persecution and oppression is persuasive evidence that Jesus Christ is alive and the guarantor of the church's survival.

But if the church is a sign of the kingdom, it is an ambiguous one. There is much in its history which obscures all that Jesus said and did. In the first place, since the Enlightenment, Christian belief has been increasingly privatized. The salvation of the individual soul has been thought to be its only proper concern. But in recent years this has been widely seen to be a truncation of the gospel. Even in evangelical circles where the privatization of religion has been and still is prevalent, there has been an awakening to the implications of the gospel for the ordering of public affairs. The mainstream churches have on the whole recognized this, and their departments of social responsibility have sought to bring Christian insights to bear on current political, social, and economic issues, both national and international. There have been notable occasions when this has led to public pronouncements challenging the authority and power of the state, such as the Barmen Declaration of the Confessional Church during the Hitler regime in Germany (to which I have already referred) and the *Kairos* document of the South African churches rejecting the apartheid system in the light of the gospel. Reference may also be made to the carefully researched report of the Church of England entitled *Faith in the City*, which drew fresh attention to the plight of those who live at the heart of our large conurbations. But as long as the privatization of Christianity remains the hallmark of so many of its members, the prophetic sign of the church is compromised and its message muted.

The second source of ambiguity is the division within the church itself. When the question has been asked, "What has the church got to say about this public issue?" the only possible response has been "Which church?" Moreover, the divisions within the church have themselves been an affront to the gospel, which has to do with the reconciliation of all people and all things in Christ. "Is Christ divided?" asked the apostle Paul in his letter to Corinth, where divisions between Christians had already become a serious problem (1 Cor. 1:13). When churches confront one another or compete with one another, they are denying the gospel that they claim to profess. Happily, in recent years, particularly since the Second Vatican Council in the early 1960s, the situation has markedly changed as Christians have come increasingly to acknowledge that they belong to one another, sharing the same faith in Jesus Christ as Lord. Whatever their differences in liturgy and doctrine, their common faith binds them to one another, and they have come to recognize that this unity must find expression so that "the world may believe" (John 17:21).

Thus at the end of World War II, the World Council of Churches, headquartered in Geneva, came into being, and it became possible to speak of the reality of the World Church, what Archbishop William Temple described in his enthronement sermon as "the great new fact of our time." And in every country, councils of churches have been established to coordinate the witness of Christians in every place. In September 1990, new instruments of ecumenism were set up in England, Scotland, Ireland, and Wales in which the Roman Catholic and black-led churches agreed to participate not as strangers but as fellow pilgrims on the road to closer unity. September 1990 marked the beginning of pledged commitment to one another as a clear move beyond the growing cooperation of the preceding years. On the first Sunday of the month following the services of inauguration, every congregation throughout the land was asked to join in a solemn act of commitment to and prayer for these new relationships that had been given national expression.

Of course there is a long way to go. Many Christians are still wedded to their sectarian ghettos and fearful that closer relationship with those who differ from them in matters of doctrine threaten their cherished beliefs and practices; and some will cynically point to Northern Ireland and its tribal conflict with religious overtones as evidence that Christianity is a divisive force rather than a uniting bond. But even in that troubled part of the world the churches on both sides of the political divide are working together for reconciliation, even if this does not get the publicity that the latest terrorist outrage attracts. Ecumenism markedly overshadows sectarianism, which is the preserve of those who continue to think that their own limited grasp of the truth is the bulwark they must defend at all costs, shutting their eyes to the possibility that God may be challenging them to a larger vision. At the celebration inaugurating the new Council of Churches in Britain and Ireland in the Anglican Cathedral at Liverpool, prior to the procession of the vast congregation to the nearby Roman Catholic cathedral, the Moderator of the Free Churches wryly remarked in his sermon, "Some of our ancestors will be protesting in the streets who have not awoken to the fact that peace has broken out." The signs of reconciliation and growing unity in service and mission are there to be seen by those who have eyes to discern what is happening. Is this simply a piece of ecclesiastical manipulation or evidence of the activity of God and the breaking through of his kingdom? Those who were celebrating at Liverpool had no doubt about the answer.

These developments may be read as signs of the kingdom of God in a world that appears to be disintegrating in hostility and conflict. But the shame of past and present divisions in the church, which is all that many people seem to know about and which is placarded whenever the media report the sectarian and tribal divisions in Northern Ireland, casts a shadow over the church's witness to unity and reconciliation. And the shadow is darkened by the continued adherence to divisive ecclesiastical structures that impede the progress toward Christian unity. The churches have still got a long way to go before they will be clearly seen as an unequivocal sign of the kingdom of God.

The third reason for seeing the church as an ambiguous sign of the kingdom is the hesitation that increasing numbers of Christians feel about claiming the moral authority of the church in a pluralist society. Its members, though still numerous, constitute only a minority of the population. What authority can they claim when so many others do not accept their beliefs, either professing another religious loyalty or looking for moral standards elsewhere on a purely secular basis? Surely, it is argued, the most we can hope for is some kind of consensus on the values to which a given society can appeal and in the light of which legislation can be enacted.

That seems obvious provided it is taken for granted that there are various religious and secular options between which people can choose according to their inclinations. It rests on the assumption that Christianity, Judaism, Islam, Hinduism, Buddhism, secularism, and all other interpretations of the world are humanly devised ideologies that have no necessary grounding in things as they are. But when it comes to matters of fact and what is true, there are not options in this sense. We cannot choose to accept whether there are daffodils growing at the bottom of my garden or whether my hand will be burnt if I put it in the fire. I may ignore the fact or believe it to be a hallucination. But if it is a fact, that is not altered by my attitude toward it. I have contended that Christianity is based on a crucial fact: that the world was redeemed by Jesus and the kingdom of God inaugurated by his advent. If that is so, then Christians must proclaim it, no matter what other people believe.

This does not entitle the church to be triumphalist, as it has often sadly been in the past. Nor have Christians any right to dominate others or insist that they subject themselves to the authority they proclaim. That is precluded by the nature of the gospel and the way God exercises his sovereignty. Human freedom must always be respected. Furthermore, Christians have no reason to say that adherents of other faiths may not have insights into the purpose of God and have genuine knowledge of him. I shall return to this theme, which has been the subject of so much debate in recent years. But here I want to insist that there is no need for hesitation in proclaiming the gospel as the ultimate truth of what God has done and is doing, always provided it is presented with sensitivity and due regard for the freedom of others that God himself respects.

Fourth, and closely related to what I have just said, the ambiguity of the church is often manifest in the weakening hold on and lack of confidence in the gospel that Christians are committed to proclaim. Within the churches of all denominations there has been and is a tendency to base faith on human experience rather than on the given and objective nature of that on which faith depends. Liberal and postliberal theologians have talked as if religion in general and Christianity in particular were systems of belief devised by human imagination. The end of that road is the kind of religion that Don Cupitt advocates, in which we would be confined to our own aspirations and wishful thinking without any grounding in a realm that transcends our thoughts. There are those who do not go as far as this but start in the same place and claim that transcendent values impinge on our experience and that therefore we can begin to reconstruct the Christian faith without dependence on the basis to which the apostolic church bore witness; they are open to the question of whether they have anything credible to say. John Bowden is one of those whose presuppositions and conclusions I have in mind. But he ends the book to which I have earlier referred with a moving confession of faith, a conviction that we have to go on living with questions and a call for reformation and action within the church. However, it is far from clear on what foundation such action should be based. For my part, I have to say that if the gospel of the kingdom is a myth and simply represents the impulse of a search for God activated by Jesus, I would have to be much more radical than Bowden and those who adopt a similar position: I would have to abandon the quest altogether. I say this with due regard for the integrity and honesty of those whom I am criticizing, but I believe that abandonment of the givenness of the gospel and denial that it is based on objective fact not only question the church as a sign of the kingdom but issue in a dead end. Theology should always be open to questions, and the interpretation of the Faith should always be a developing process, but these things must be grounded on what is ultimately given to carry conviction. Confusion about this is a serious malaise that is clouding and compromising the church's witness to the kingdom.

There is much else to be said about the ambiguity of the church. So far I have been speaking mainly about its failure of fidelity in witness to the gospel. But that is further compromised by the way in which it orders ecclesiastical affairs and the image it presents. It was inevitable that as Christianity spread and congregations were founded in many places, the church should become organized.

Institutions come into being whenever people are committed to a common purpose, but then they are in constant danger of becoming fossilized, concerned with their self-preservation and the vested interests of those who control them. In the church, the proliferation of bureaucracy with its councils, synods, and committees can easily become an end in itself, and that frequently gives the impression that the church is introverted, occupied more with its own internal structure than with its mission to the world. Of course, every institution is subject to the same criticism, but there can be little doubt that in the perception of many people the church is compromised by its preoccupation with its own organization.

Those who are engaged at all levels in maintaining the institutions in which they have become involved are likely to feel frustrated and irritated by such criticism. They are almost without exception people of integrity who are committed to serving God in his church and engaging in his mission to the world. But they are caught up in what they have inherited, and this is a male and clerically dominated institution, one which is resistant to change and in which the vested interests keeping it such are insidiously pervasive.

One of the most striking things about all church councils is the very small number of women to be found in their membership. That is obviously the case with the Roman Catholic and Anglican churches. Even those churches that are more open to feminine leadership and lay participation, with a number of women ordained as ministers, are still predominantly male and clerically led. This reflects what is also true of society at large. For example, while Britain has had a woman prime minister, the rest of her cabinet were all men. The United States has never had a woman president, and only a comparative handful of women occupy seats in the Congress. The same relative proportion is the case in business, industry, and the professions. But it is probably the case that there are more doors open to women in the secular world than in the church, which is seen to be trailing behind the rest of society and more entrenched in male prejudice.

The feminist movement is a growing protest against this situation, and feminist theologians are beginning to make their voices heard, calling for a radical rethinking of the relationship between women and men in light of the gospel. This is much wider than the current controversy about the ordination of women priests and ministers. In a recent symposium of articles by feminist theologians, edited by Dr. Grace Jantzen of King's College London, the claim is made that feminist theology will present the greatest challenge the church has to face in the years ahead.[1]

The stridency of some of the protests has raised hackles in many quarters, and some feminists seem to be unable to understand the reaction to them of large numbers of women who do not feel oppressed and angry as they do. To say that these women ought to feel oppressed and that they are simply burying their heads in the sand violates the sincere convictions and contradicts the experience of many of those with whom militant feminists do not agree. Discovering the right relationship between women and men in the purpose of God is a complex problem that needs to take into full account the complementarity of the sexes. Women and men are constituted differently and in general have different gifts. The undertones, often overtones, of unisex thinking vitiate the whole debate.

My credentials for venturing to enter into the discussion at all may be explained by the unusual experience that I was privileged to have in my early years. On my ordination in 1938, I joined the full-time staff of twenty or more at the West Ham Central Mission in East London. Women outnumbered men there by at least three to one, and the ministry was jointly led by my mother and father, who had founded the Mission. There was no doubt that my mother was the predominant partner, though the two complemented each other in a remarkable way. There was never any question, as far as I remember, of sexual discrimination in the ministry of the whole

1. *Theology* 93, no. 775, September/October 1990 (SPCK).

staff. The experience of this lay behind my father's presidential address to the Baptist Union Assembly in Glasgow in 1933, when he took as his theme the need to find ways of implementing the full participation of women in the ministry and mission of the church. Half a century later, one of the few women on the Baptist Union Council referred to this address with the words "How long, O Lord? How long?" Indeed, the time is long overdue for the churches of all denominations to take this issue seriously. Until they do, and exhibit a real and complementary partnership grounded in a theological rethinking of the tradition, they will be seen as obscuring the gospel addressed to all people.

Clerical control of church structures is parallel to their dominance by males. This control is particularly insidious because the clergy do have a vested interest as paid professionals in keeping things as they are. They subtly tend to see themselves as the church, and certainly they are so perceived by the population at large, and that despite lip service given to the true church as being the whole people of God. Of course, the ordained ministry of those set apart for the preaching of the Word of God, the administration of the sacraments, and pastoral care is essential to the church's ministry. But much of the discussion about it does not center on their role *within* the people of God; rather, it focuses on their role in itself. In the Anglican Church, arguments about the proper method of ordination and the necessity of preserving the threefold hierarchy of bishop, priest, and deacon have become such a major preoccupation that they have tended to take precedence over all other issues of the church's mission, and one suspects that nontheological considerations about status and prestige play an all-too-important part beneath the genuine theological issues at stake. Moreover, it is important to realize that the heated controversy about the ordination of women priests and ministers is but a facet of this preoccupation. However the controversy is resolved in the Anglican Church, the fact that it appears to take the center of the stage may be not only the tip of the iceberg of the feminist challenge to the status quo, but also an indication of the lack of proportion in the church's over-preoccupation with its ordained ministry. This is how many Christians tend to see it, and members of the general public are inclined to think of it as not very interesting or important and as evidence of the church's preoccupation with its own internal affairs.

It will be very difficult to change this lack of a sense of proportion and the image of clerical dominance. It will happen only as the ministry of the laity comes to be taken seriously, and they cease to be regarded as second-class Christian citizens. This was the theme of a book published some years ago entitled *God's Frozen People*.[2] It was a passionate plea for recognizing the mission of the laity as central to the coming of God's kingdom. Until that is the focus of Christian concern and compels the ordained ministry to see its enabling role within the whole people of God, the church will continue to be an ambiguous sign of the kingdom.

At the local level, the image of the church is still further seriously distorted and obscured. Many congregations in cities, towns, and villages are little more than religious clubs primarily concerned with preserving their buildings, often long past their utility to the members, and continuing the customs with which they have become familiar. The idea that they should share their resources with their fellow Christians in the same place and turn outward to the needs of the community around them often meets with dogged resistance; it is a threat to the club. This outlook, if that is what it can be called, is particularly prevalent in the Free Churches in Britain. The Anglican equivalent is the model of the corner shop, where the incumbent administers the rites of passage at birth, marriage, and death to those who ask for them and conducts services for the few who choose to attend, services that the average person would not begin to understand.

2. Mark Gibbs and Ralph Morton, *God's Frozen People* (Collins–Fontana, 1964).

But even when the local church presents the most drab and dreary image, there is another side to the picture. Among its membership are likely to be those whose lives have been shaped by their faith in Jesus Christ and who exert a considerable influence among their neighbors and friends. This was brilliantly illustrated by C. S. Lewis in *The Screwtape Letters,* where the chief of the temptation department in hell gives advice to his nephew, who has just taken up the job of a junior tempter, on how to deal with someone who has begun to take Christianity seriously and has his first encounter with the local church. "All your patient sees is the half-finished, sham Gothic erection on the new building estate. When he goes inside, he sees the local grocer with rather an oily expression on his face bustling up to offer him one shiny little book containing a liturgy which neither of them understands, and one shabby little book containing corrupt texts of a number of religious lyrics, mostly bad, and in very small print. When he gets to his pew and looks round him he sees just that selection of his neighbours whom he has hitherto avoided. You want to lean heavily on those neighbours. Make his mind flit to and fro between an expression like 'the body of Christ' and the actual faces in the next pew. It matters very little, of course, what kind of people that next pew really contains. You may know one of them to be a great warrior on the Enemy's side."[3] In spite of members like this, many local congregations are a travesty of what the church is meant to be.

There is still another side to the picture where a quite different image is presented. Our beautiful cathedrals and historic churches eloquently speak of the desire to glorify God and offer to his praise the best in music, art, and craftsmanship. And there are many parishes and congregations where vitality and genuine Christian fellowship are to be found, and where there is an outward-looking approach in service to the community of which they are part. All

3. Lewis, *The Screwtape Letters* (Bles, 1942), pp. 15-16.

the same, the church presents an ambiguous image, often enslaved to old ways and imprisoned in hidebound structures. It seems far from the apostle's vision of it as presented "all glorious, with no stain or wrinkle or anything of the sort, but holy and without blemish" (Eph. 5:27). Nevertheless, it is a sign: a continuing testimony to the kingdom of God throughout the ages. An ambiguous sign? Yes. But a powerful one all the same.

CHAPTER TEN

Signs of the Kingdom

Those who remain unconvinced that the church is an authentic sign of the reality of the kingdom of God have still to face the evidence of the change in human lives through faith in the crucified and risen Christ and the impact this has made on society in general. Christians have no monopoly on virtue. They are sinful men and women who acknowledge every time they come to church that they fall far short of the glory of God. The only claim they make is that they are what they are through faith in Christ and what he has done for them. Christians are often compared with those who make no profession of such faith, adherents of other religions and humanists, the quality of whose lives and contribution to the common good compare more than favorably with that of many Christians. But that is not the point. The only valid claim that Christians are entitled to make is that they owe what they are to faith in Jesus Christ.

Comparisons are odious, particularly when they are made between one person and another. We are all so very different, with differences of upbringing, gifts, and social conditioning. The only valid comparison is between what anyone is and what he or she might be or might have been, and that depends in large part on the beliefs and values he or she cherishes. What is or should be the characteristic of a Christian is the way in which allegiance to Christ and acknowledgment of him as Lord shapes and influences his or her life.

The first thing that identifies a Christian is the recognition of being a sinner dependent on the mercy and grace of God. Those who depend on themselves and their moral achievements may well be courageous and virtuous, but they also may be lacking any radical self-criticism. Jesus said that repentance was the prerequisite for entering the kingdom of God, and he underlined this in the parable of the Pharisee and the publican. It was the one who said "God be merciful to me a sinner" who was declared justified before God (Luke 18:13-14, KJV). This is true or false, realistic or unrealistic. But if we look around us and see where human pretensions to unaided achievement have led us, it is difficult to resist the conclusion that human beings are fatally flawed and infected by what Christians have called original sin, the state of corporate rebellion against God in which we are all involved. If this is the real state of affairs, the foundation for any credible reformation of life is repentance.

Second, Christians, whoever they may be, are to be judged by their relationship to their Lord and the influence this has on the lives they live. Whatever the motivations of others, there can be no doubt that the distinctive mark of Christians is this relationship and allegiance. It determines their concern for other people and their service to the community at large. It is nourished by joining in worship and receiving the sacrament of Holy Communion, in which Christians claim to meet with God and receive from him both their commission and the resources to discharge it. They would not be what they are without this divine encounter and the grace given in it.

Evidence of this can be seen in the lives of many who make striking contributions to the welfare of their fellow men and women and frankly own their inspiration to Jesus Christ. We have only to think of Mother Theresa, with her care for the orphans, the outcasts, and the unwanted in Calcutta and elsewhere throughout the world;

or Cecily Saunders, the founder of hospices for those suffering terminal illnesses; or Bishop Romero, shot to death in El Salvador because of his championship of the poor; or Archbishop Tutu, who has fought against apartheid and campaigned for reconciliation between the races in South Africa.

These are people who, without intending to do so, catch the public eye and become widely known. But there are countless others whose names never appear in the newspapers and whose faces are never seen on the television screen who in various ways serve their fellows in the name of Christ and whose lives exhibit the winsomeness of the grace of God. Where would our voluntary services be without them? What would society be like if the influence of Jesus were to be removed from both public and private life? I have already referred to Augustine's letter to Marcellinus in the fifth century in which he made the same point in reply to the criticism that Christianity was inimical to the welfare of the state.[1] With a great many others, I find the most convincing sign of the kingdom in the lives of those I have known who, despite admitted failures, mirror the Christ whom they serve.

Some of those reading the foregoing paragraphs may have become mountingly irritated with them. In spite of what I have already said about Christians having no monopoly on virtue, my comments may be taken as veiled claims to superiority. That would be a misunderstanding of what I have been trying to say. The point I have been making is that Christians are different in that whatever virtue they exhibit is based upon repentance and conversion in the face of God's judgment[2] and dependence on the grace of God in Jesus Christ. Certainly there are innumerable examples of sheer goodness among those who are adherents of other religions and among humanists as well. To say this is not patronizing, nor is it

1. See *supra,* p. 72.
2. See Rowan Williams, *supra* p. 46.

meant to be. If we believe in God, we must say that wherever goodness is to be found, it is due to his inspiration, whether or not that is recognized. God's activity is not confined to Christians or the adherents of any other religion. He is providentially at work in the whole world if he is active anywhere. According to the apostle Paul, "The fruit of the Spirit is love, joy, peace, longsuffering, gentleness, goodness, faith, meekness, temperance" (Gal. 5:22-23). There are numerous people who display these qualities, sometimes to a marked degree, and that in contrast to all the meanness, selfishness, pettiness, and sheer maliciousness all around them. The prevalence of goodness is as much a problem as evil, if not a greater one. It is a fact that calls out for explanation. Those who display goodness are evidence of God's kingdom, which extends far beyond the bounds of the Christian church.

The influence of Jesus is not restricted to the quality of the lives of those who claim allegiance to him. It is reflected in the many great works of art that are an essential part of our heritage. The cathedrals of Europe with their towering spires and Gothic arches, their sculpture and carving, speak of him. So do the paintings devoted to the themes of his life, death, and resurrection, as do the works of great composers like Johann Sebastian Bach. Those who have performed or listened sensitively to such masterpieces as the *Mass in B Minor* and the *St. Matthew Passion* cannot fail to have been moved by the experience, which has enabled them to discern something of the glory of God and the wonder of redemption that words alone cannot convey. What would have been the loss to our cultural heritage if Jesus had never lived, and if architects, craftsmen, painters, poets, writers, and musicians had not been captured by the story of his life and been inspired by the creative impulse of the Spirit he promised to give?

There are other signs of the kingdom that undergird what I have said so far about the testimony of individual Christian lives and the contribution of great artists. One of those engaged in the group of biblical specialists to which I referred in the preface was James Dunn, the New Testament professor at the University of Durham. He brought together a group of academics and those engaged in a variety of practical projects in the northeast of England to see the extent to which the New Testament vision of the kingdom illuminated and informed what they were doing. The result was a paperback the heart of which consisted of twelve case studies contributed by those seeking to put their faith into practice.[3] The case studies detailed attempts to meet the needs of the unemployed and mentally handicapped; a successful campaign to preserve a village school and its place within the community; a cooperative venture in curriculum planning in education at the secondary level; a fair-trade shop in an industrial town; the redeployment of the resources of a monastery and an inner-city church; and turning a hermitage into a contemplative community. In what sense were these signs of the kingdom?

To some extent they could obviously be claimed to be such. They were practical expressions of genuine Christian concern. But in the discussion following publication by the original group that sponsored the project, some searching questions were asked. In particular, Professor Ronald Preston, while giving a general welcome to the book, said that he did not believe it really came to terms with the fact that Christians have to live in two kingdoms: the kingdom of God and the kingdom of this world. To what extent were these case studies examples of radically grappling with the actual secular situations in which Christians find themselves involved? It is obviously laudable and greatly to be encouraged that local congregations, especially in urban areas, should emerge from their ghettos and endeavor to see how their resources can be put at the service of the community. But when they become engaged in ambulance work for the unemployed or the handicapped, are they really coming to terms with the ambiguity in which they are involved?

3. Dunn, *The Kingdom of God and North East England* (SCM, 1986).

Such was the substance of Professor Preston's critique. It does not undervalue the case studies in question as signs of the kingdom, but it requires us to go further and face the ambiguities of witness in secular institutions where Christians find themselves involved in decisions and practices in which those who do not accept their values or who are unwilling to take them seriously have the influential voice. This applies to business, industry, politics, and the professions. If life is to go on, compromises have to be made, but it is extremely difficult to determine where the line is to be drawn between rejection of the enterprise because it so obviously violates Christian values and settling for the best that can be done in the circumstances. There are cases — for instance, in the promotion of pornography — where the issue is clear. For the most part, however, the Christian responsibility is to stick with the job and act as leaven in the lump. That too may be a powerful, albeit ambiguous, sign of the kingdom.

Unhappily, however, many choose to take the easy way out. They withdraw into Bible study and prayer groups which meet in hospitals, schools, places of business, and elsewhere, and which are primarily concerned with the nurture of the spiritual life and unrelated to the jobs they are paid to do. But there are others who try to take seriously their Christian responsibilities in the secular occupations in which they are involved. For example, the vicar in a Surrey parish invited those working for multinational corporations to meet as a group and share their problems and experience in the light of the faith they professed. Initiatives of this kind are sadly rare, and many, particularly among those carrying heavy public responsibilities, feel suffocated in the churches to which they belong, lacking the opportunity to explore the relation of their faith to what they have to do every day. As one of the leaders of British industry confessed to me in conversation, "What I hear from the pulpit on Sunday morning is of no help to me during the week and seems to have nothing to do with it." The signs of the kingdom are thereby muted. Some words of the late Canon Grenstead are very much to the point: "I am not so concerned with the defence of the Christian Sunday as I am with the conquest of the pagan week!"

We need to go still further. Are there signs of the kingdom in those situations where evil appears to have triumphed and God's purposes are frustrated or openly defied? If God is sovereign over the whole universe, can we discern signs of his kingdom in floods, earthquakes, and famines, in concentration and refugee camps, in the war-torn Middle East, or in structures dominated by violence and greed? If not, then it is questionable whether we can discern them anywhere else. That brings us back to the central thesis of this book. "Only a suffering God can help," wrote Bonhoeffer from prison as he faced execution by the Nazis.[4] He is and he does, as many have testified in passing through the vale of suffering. "Though I walk through the valley of the shadow of death," said the Psalmist, "I will fear no evil: for thou art with me; thy rod and thy staff they comfort me" (23:4, KJV). The Christian conviction is that at the heart of human history stands the cross from which Jesus reigns, the conqueror of sin, suffering, and death, and promises his victorious presence to those who tread the same path.

It is more difficult to grasp this because we are mesmerized by numbers. In the end, the crux of human pain, suffering, and death, as Rowan Williams said in his essay to which I have already referred, is focused in one individual. It is simply multiplied in the traumas and tragedies of large numbers of people who are affected at the same time as one another. The question we have to ask is whether there can be signs of the power of the cross and resurrection in the experience of *any* individual and whether this is the clue to how things ultimately are.

There are many examples to which we might look. Some of these may perhaps be found in the experiences of triumph over suffering and death in the hospices for the terminally ill founded

4. Bonhoeffer, *Letters and Papers from Prison* (SCM, 1953).

by Dame Cecily Saunders. My own wife spent the last weeks of her life in the Sobel wing of the Churchill Hospital at Oxford. She had suffered for four years from cancer, which spread from her breast to her lungs, to her spine, and finally back to her lungs, which necessitated surgery for a tracheostomy to enable her to breathe artificially through a tube. This was the last straw, and she was dreadfully afraid of the immediate future and how she could face the way in which her life was ending. She was admitted to the Sobel wing to be cared for by those who shared a wonderful faith in the love and power of God. For five weeks I saw the power of the spirit overcoming the rapid weakening of the body, dispelling all fear and leading to a triumphant death inspired by faith in the crucified and risen Lord.

This kind of experience could be multiplied many times over in the face of many different circumstances. We have only to think of Bonhoeffer awaiting execution in prison at the hands of Nazis, of the innumerable examples of heroism and self-sacrifice in circumstances of disaster, of those whose names are unknown who have discovered the power of the crucified and risen Lord in conditions of appalling calamity. Of course, there are many counter-examples that could be quoted. Innumerable men, women, and children have suffered and died without faith and hope, many embittered or fatalistic or simply despairing about their lot. But the question must be pressed whether the fact that even one example of the triumph of faith in the face of suffering, disaster, and death is without significance. In the end it may be of ultimate significance, pointing to how things really are in a universe that otherwise seems utterly meaningless.

The Christian gospel has sometimes been described as the scandal of particularity: the belief that one event involving one human being is decisive for everybody and indeed for the whole universe. For Christians, that one ultimately decisive event is the crucifixion and resurrection of Jesus. Signs that this is the truth may be discerned in every particular experience of triumph through faith in him and as ultimately redeeming every tragedy, even of those who suffer and die without faith or hope.

The cross may be a scandal, a stumbling block, and sheer foolishness to many today just as much as it was when Paul proclaimed it in the first century. But the fact that it has, in the words of the hymn, "towered o'er the wrecks of time" still carries the conviction that it is "the power of God, and the wisdom of God" (1 Cor. 1:24), the crucial evidence that God reigns.

CHAPTER ELEVEN

The End of the Twentieth Century

As we approach the year 2000, anyone who thinks seriously is bound to ask what the prospects are for the human race in the next century. What chances are there for survival for another hundred years, let alone another millennium? When Desmond King-Hele wrote his book *The End of the Twentieth Century* (to which I referred earlier), it was at the height of the Cold War, and then it looked to him, according to a probability calculation, that it was unlikely we would survive until the year 2000. But he ended with the hope that somehow we would muddle through.

Since then, the danger he foresaw has somewhat receded. The superpowers were on the brink of the abyss at the time of the Cuban crisis and drew back, and the dramatic changes in the Soviet Union and Eastern Europe have removed still further the threat of imminent global catastrophe. But thermonuclear weapons remain stockpiled, and in any case they cannot be disinvented. If those who possess them were to forswear their manufacture and use altogether, there might still be a dictator in one of the smaller countries or a desperate terrorist group who would get hold of them and not hesitate to use them if driven into a corner. The fear of that possibility was certainly one of the things which led to the massive deployment of military power in the Gulf in the face of Saddam Hussein's invasion of Kuwait.

Nevertheless, the specter of rampant nationalism compounded by racial and tribal conflict lies behind the international arms trade, in which powerful interests are vested. Nationalism may be obsolete in an increasingly interdependent world, but it shows no sign of diminishing. For example, moves toward closer unity in Europe run into resistance from entrenched interests, not least when the freedom of action of a national government or sectional privileges within a country seem to be in danger of being curtailed. If this was not enough, the pollution of the environment and the exploitation of scarce resources have forced their way to the top of the political agenda. A few years ago hardly anyone, except those in small pressure groups, took the problem seriously. Today no politician can afford to neglect the challenge. It cannot be put off, as once it vaguely was, to some distant future. Unless action is taken now and the myth of indefinite economic expansion at any cost to the natural environment is exploded, not only the long-term but also the short-term prospects for human welfare are bleak indeed.

One further crucial factor has to be taken into account. As we look back over the last hundred years, we are bound to be struck by the extraordinary changes that have taken place and the speed with which they have occurred compared with the rate of change in the relatively stable societies of the preceding centuries. To quote from the chapter of a book which I wrote in the 1970s and which I see no reason to alter from subsequent experience, we feel like people on an escalator that never stops. "When you step on to an escalator at an underground station, you know whether you are going up or down and that you will be on firm ground in a matter of moments. Imagine finding yourself on an endless escalator, unable to get off, with no idea whether you are going up or down or in any direction whatever, and certain only that all the time you are gathering speed. That would be a terrifying nightmare, but it is not too far-fetched an illustration of our human predicament in the bewildering period of history through which we are living."[1]

The late Professor Charles A. Coulson described the pace of change during his own lifetime in a lecture he gave at Luton Industrial College:

> Nearly three hundred and fifty years ago people began seriously to study the behavior of magnets . . . but it took us no less than two hundred and fifty years until Professor James Clerk Maxwell was able to give a sufficiently good account of this whole field that it became a fully usable phenomenon. . . . In the post-war era it took only three years from the discovery . . . that a wireless valve could be replaced by a transistor before these little things had developed to such an extent that not only were they on the public market, but in one year their sale amounted to almost exactly the same as that of the valve they were replacing.[2]

350-250-3-1. That was the accelerating pace of change in one limited field, and examples could be multiplied over and over again, not least in the years that have followed Charles Coulson's lecture. One is led to wonder whether human beings can go on adjusting to such a pace. It is plainly all too much for many people, who in increasing numbers break down, unable to cope with the strain and stress to which they are subjected.

The speed of change is compounded for vast numbers of people by the sheer size of our institutions and the magnitude of the problems that confront us. Moreover, we often feel overpowered by the sense of our insignificance "as specks upon a speck of dust in a vast universe that defies our imagination. We may be able to forget

---

1. Clifford, *The Death of the Dinosaur* (SPCK, 1977), p. 1.
2. Coulson, *Faith and Technology* (Methodist Publishing House, 1969), pp. 8-9.

the immense physical context in which we live out our lives for a brief span of years, but we still have to come to terms with a human environment which seems to be completely beyond our control. The vast conurbations, with their high-rise apartment blocks in which increasing numbers find themselves absorbed, tend to dwarf the individual and reduce him or her to a cipher. For many this is accentuated by the factories and institutions for which they work. Multi-national corporations, disposing of the livelihood of thousands of employees from remote centres of control, reduce them to little more than cogs in the machines they operate. The growing power of the state, with its mushrooming bureaucracy, makes people feel that they no longer count except as statistics to be manipulated by faceless officials. . . . Even the health, welfare, and education services have become so big and so complex that the ordinary person comes more and more to believe that he or she has to take what they are given without any say in the kind of provision that is made for them."[3] The result is that the majority tend to give up and retire into a private world of the transitory present without any rootage in the past or real hope for the future. "Sceptical of the promises of politicians, who seem to have lost control of events as they jump from one expedient to another, and lacking any real faith in the future, the average person confines himself to getting as much satisfaction as he can out of the passing show. His job, his family, his circle of friends and his recreation make up his world: here today and gone tomorrow."[4] But in the end nobody can escape the ultimate questions. Even if we refuse to think about them, we are in practice settling for one of the answers: life is meaningless, and we have to accept our fate.

It is impossible to predict the future, but at least we can come to terms with the options available to us as we make our way through

3. Clifford, *The Death of the Dinosaur,* pp. 6-7.
4. Clifford, *The Death of the Dinosaur,* pp. 5-6.

the last decade of this century and look to the dawn of the next. One of those options is atheistic secularism. This has obviously been spreading in Europe and to a lesser extent in North America since World War I. Its most optimistic expression was in the old Soviet Union, which officially adopted and propagated the dogmas of economic determinism and Marx's belief in the inevitability of progress to a classless society. We have seen this ideology dramatically collapse from its own internal contradictions, and even those who have believed that they could correct its errors and replace it with the goal of democratic socialism have begun to find that this does not so credibly fit the realities of economics or the aspirations of ordinary people. Atheistic secularists have been stripped of their dreams of progress, if they happened to have had them — and not all of them by any means did — and face the stark reality that life is ultimately meaningless, that the human race has no future or at best a very precarious one, and that all we can do is accept our fate and make what we can of our lives in the brief time allotted to us.

This is a perfectly credible option, and there is much evidence to support it. Those who adopt it may simply appear to be cynics, but they are often courageous people who are prepared to face the facts as they see them. However, it is important to be clear about what this option really is and not try to mitigate it or to escape from it by clouding it with confusion. This is what happens when anyone shies away from the stark consequence of meaninglessness and within the framework of atheist presuppositions seeks to find some significance in human existence.

However, there is an alternative that has come to be increasingly accepted in Western society. Its twin pillars are freedom and pluralism. Those who find that they cannot accept the nihilistic conclusions of the first option and have to make a place for our cultural heritage and the values that have informed it settle for a society in which all flowers are encouraged to bloom. In this society, all religions are given the opportunity to flourish, and people are free to pursue whatever goals they wish, provided their objectives do not impede or override one another. Tolerance should be the watchword of such a society, and all people should be free to find their satisfaction in whatever interests them. This has the advantage of turning religion into a private affair for those so inclined, leaving others free to pursue secular goals.

This is an attractive picture on the surface. But it is flawed because it involves suspending questions of truth — how things actually are — and grounding values in human aspirations. To reply that questions of truth are not suspended for scientists ignores the fact that scientists cannot be isolated from the rest of the community and that the values they adopt, whether they do so consciously or not, control the research they undertake and the effects of its outcome. But it is the source and grounding of values that present the greatest problem for the pluralist. If they spring solely from the desires and aspirations of human beings, the question arises of why we should accept anyone else's values, and the attempt to arrive at some sort of consensus may well provoke a reaction from those who challenge the authority of anybody to legislate their behavior. As I argued earlier, the whole notion of freedom becomes problematic unless it is defined in terms of responsibility, and that contradicts the presumption that we should all be our own masters.

Theories of the state and social organization have been invoked to provide some sort of cohesion where freedom to do what you like is regarded as the basic value. A distinction has been drawn between public morality, which is embodied in laws and regulations, and private morality, which is the expression of any ideal a person chooses to adopt. But the two cannot be kept apart. When freedom and pluralism are taken to be the basic criteria for the shaping of future society, chaotic consequences are bound to follow. We are beginning to see this in the materialistic aims that people are encouraged to pursue. The quantity of money and possessions that anyone can accumulate is counted as evidence of success. Economic growth takes precedence over improving the quality of life. The rich become richer and the poor poorer, and the seeds of disintegration are sown in both the individual and society. Many are beginning to look for a valid and cohesive moral basis on which society can develop. It is not to be found in competing and conflicting aspirations and desires.

If I had to choose between the two ways of understanding the human condition, I would have to settle for the first as more realistic, although more pessimistic. The second had some plausibility as long as Marxism held the field with its hope of better things to come. But with the bankruptcy of that ideology, the prospect of a radically pluralist society looks bleak, to say the least. It cannot be rescued by saying that it holds open religion as a private option; for unless religion is grounded in how things actually are and provides a firm standard for the conduct of both public and private life, it is simply one among many ideologies that have their source in a variety of human aspirations. The differences within the world's religious systems themselves become options that anyone can take or leave as they wish.

This pluralistic point of view makes it very difficult for most people in the West to begin to understand Islam. With the collapse of communism, it has suddenly come to take the center of the stage on the international scene, and it clearly has to be reckoned with as a major challenge in the years ahead. Dominant in the countries of the Middle East, Islam has taken root in many parts of Africa, is entrenched on the Indian subcontinent, and has become one of the most turbulent factors in the ethnic unrest in the former Soviet Union. Nearer home, immigrant Muslims have established their own communities in European cities, and it is no longer possible to think of them as belonging to a culture far removed from our own.

Islam is not monolithic. It is divided into competing and sometimes warring factions, as became plain in the Iran-Iraq conflict in the 1980s. But these can become submerged, if not reconciled, when the Muslim faith itself is perceived to be under attack. Common to them all is the belief in one God whose authentic prophet was Muhammad, and the belief that the sacred writings in the *Qur'an* are God's final and decisive word not only to Muslims but also to the whole of humankind. This means that Islam is a missionary religion and sometimes a militant one when a holy war or *jihad* against the infidel is declared to undergird fervent nationalist ambitions. We saw how Islam can take over a secular state when Islamic fundamentalists under the Ayatolla Khomeini ousted the Shah in Iran; when this sort of fundamentalism becomes expansionist, it poses a serious threat to world peace.

Of course, there are pragmatists in the countries dominated by Islam who see that accommodation must be reached with other nations and peoples who do not accept the Muslim faith. Moreover, there are many devout Muslims who look for dialogue and mutual understanding between those of different religious persuasions. An example of this is the Centre for the Study of Islam and Christian-Muslim Relations at the Selly Oak Colleges in Birmingham, where the staff consists of an equal number of Muslim and Christian scholars, and the student body of over a hundred is encouraged to explore differences together without compromising their basic beliefs. But this and other ventures of the same kind are only a small beginning. They need to be fostered and spread if dangerous misunderstandings that fuel the fires of hostility are to be mitigated in the years ahead.

Nevertheless, the essence of the challenge of Islam to the pluralistic societies of the West has to be clearly grasped. It is a public religion in the sense that the *Qur'an* is held to legislate for the whole of life and to determine the details of the ordering of society. In no way is it conceived of as a private option or simply as the means to personal salvation. It is the cement that binds people together and provides cohesion for any community or nation. Those in the West who do think of religion as a private option that can be marginalized and excluded from the public arena are therefore liable to be shocked when they discover that the Muslims who have settled in their cities do not want to be integrated into their way of life, which the Muslims see as having no firm moral foundations. The shock becomes a disturbing challenge when the leaders of Muslim communities begin to demand their own institutions, their own schools, and even their own self-government. The implications of this have hardly begun to be understood, let alone faced.

The overwhelming majority of people in Western Europe and North America are not likely to see Islam as a religion or a way of life they would want to adopt. Their picture of it is dominated by scenes of fanatics on the television screen beating their breasts or rhythmically demonstrating their hatred of foreigners. The other face of Islam which is hidden by the excesses of the extremists is that of devout Muslims who reject all talk of a holy war and abhor violence, and whose faith depends on reverence for the sacred writings of the *Qur'an*. But that too, while it merits respect, is unlikely to convince many who have not been nurtured in an Islamic culture. It savors too much of a return to a medieval past and dependence on a written text to which more weight is given than it can stand. That is a legitimate criticism that can be leveled equally against many Christians in their attitude toward the Bible. But that attitude is an aberration, as I have argued above, and not endemic to Christianity as it is to Islam.

When all is said and done, we have to take seriously the challenge of Islam in the contemporary world, not just because of its millions of faithful adherents, but because of its valid protest against and explicit alternative to the confusions of Western society. The Muslim belief in the absolute authority and sovereignty of the one God over the whole world, which grounds the basis of a cohesive society and moral conduct in the doing of his will, is a challenge that has to be faced. It is questionable whether this can be matched without an equally coherent alternative.

Whether Christianity can offer a more persuasive alternative has been the theme of this book. I have argued that it can do so only if it returns to its roots and rejects the errors and deviations that have marred its past. Its authentic claim, like that of Islam, is to declare how things actually are: that God is the sovereign Lord of the universe and that human life and society fulfill their purpose only in obedience to his will. But there Christianity's agreement with Islam ends. The Islamic doctrine of providence, especially when it is invoked to support autocratic rule and even a holy war, flatly contradicts the way in which Jesus proclaimed that God reigns. As Jesus declared, God never imposes his will but offers his kingdom to all who are prepared to receive it. And this may entail rejection, suffering, and death. If anything is to be learned from history, it is that this is the way God has always exercised his providence.

It is hard for human beings to accept that this is a possible option for them, let alone for God. The exercise of coercive power has seemed to be the only way in which evil could be countered or human objectives be achieved. Christians themselves have succumbed to the commonly accepted view of what is obviously the case even when this has led to the destruction and devastation that has marked the course of history and disfigures the world today. Down the centuries Christians have sought to force God's hand. They engaged in the medieval Crusades. They sought to use political power to impose the dominance of the church. More subtly and often without realizing what they were doing, they became the tools of economic and cultural imperialism in the propagation of the gospel. For the most part, the churches today forswear all this and make no pretensions to political power. But the temptations remain, and all too easily the gospel can be compromised by manipulating people and situations in ways that contravene the respect for the freedom of others that proclamation of the kingdom of God demands.

The kingdom of God is realized only by persuasion, not by imposition. At the heart of its proclamation are the cross and resurrection of Jesus, which confound all human pretensions to power. This is not a prescription for passivity, still less for indifference to truth or an easygoing tolerance of pluralism. Christian claims rest on the conviction that this is how things actually are, that in the life, death, and resurrection of Jesus, the kingdom of God was established on earth and the world redeemed. This is true for everyone, whether they believe it or not. In the words of Lesslie Newbigin, "To affirm the centrality, the decisiveness, the absoluteness of this one name, is to affirm that — in the last analysis — the human story is one story, not a medley of different stories. It is to affirm that we belong together in one history and that this history has a shape, a meaning and a goal. But that affirmation can be made without incurring the accusation of imperialism only because it is made, not in the name of the Christian church, but in the name of one who reigns from the tree, the one who has made peace by the blood of the cross, the one who has alone broken the power of sin and death and pierced the barrier that divides the time of our human history from the eternal of God in whom is our home."[5]

Those who share in this conviction understand the universe and human history within it neither as meaningless nor as open to a variety of human interpretations that may be equally valid or invalid. Nor do they believe that the universe is under the dominance of an autocratic creator who exercises his omnipotence as that is commonly understood. They see it as a universe the all-embracing characteristic of which is freedom, the misuse and distortion of which are redeemed by the cross and resurrection of Jesus. They are committed to the paradoxical affirmation of the unique particularity of this event. Thus they conceive the kingdom or reign of God as established by that event within history and believe that God's redeeming love will ultimately be recognized as triumphant.

To accept this implies that the kingdom of God has to do with

5. Newbigin, "The Christian Faith and World Religions," in *Keeping the Faith,* ed. Geoffrey Wainwright (SPCK, 1989), p. 338. For a fuller exposition, cf. Newbigin, *The Gospel in a Pluralist Society* (SPCK, 1989).

the whole created order: with our stewardship of natural resources, with all forms of life on this planet, as well as with the structures of human society. Christianity is not just the promise of salvation to the individual. The individual taken alone is abstracted from relationship with other people in society and with the natural world. The gospel of the kingdom is about the transformation of the whole created universe and therefore is the touchstone by which all human decisions in the body politic are to be assessed.

Whether this is a credible option for us depends on how far it makes sense in the light of our experience. But it does offer a message of hope that, as far as I can see, all alternatives lack. If it is dismissed as wishful thinking, then I do not believe there is any realistic alternative to cynical nihilism, the view that life has no meaning and history no purpose. But for me this book must end with the confession of faith at the close of the Lord's Prayer: "Thine is the kingdom, the power, and the glory."